WESTWARD WE CAME

WESTWARD WE CAME
A NORWEGIAN IMMIGRANT'S STORY, 1866–1898

HAROLD B. KILDAHL, SR.

EDITED AND ORGANIZED
BY
ERLING E. KILDAHL

PURDUE UNIVERSITY PRESS
WEST LAFAYETTE, INDIANA

PRINTED IN THE UNITED STATES OF AMERICA

LIBRARY OF CONGRESS CATALOGING-IN-PUBLICATION DATA

KILDAHL, HAROLD B. (HAROLD BERG), 1865-1945.
  WESTWARD WE CAME : A NORWEGIAN IMMIGRANT'S STORY,
1866-1898 / HAROLD B. KILDAHL, SR. ; EDITED AND ORGANIZED BY
ERLING E. KILDAHL.
    P. CM.
  ISBN 978-1-55753-471-2
  1. KILDAHL, HAROLD B. (HAROLD BERG), 1865-1945. 2.
KILDAHL, HAROLD B. (HAROLD BERG), 1865-1945--FAMILY.
3. NORWEGIAN AMERICANS--MINNESOTA--BIOGRAPHY. 4.
PIONEERS--MINNESOTA--BIOGRAPHY. 5. FRONTIER AND PIONEER
LIFE--MINNESOTA. 6. MINNESOTA--HISTORY--19TH CENTURY.
7. FRONTIER AND PIONEER LIFE--RED RIVER VALLEY (MINN. AND
N.D.-MAN.) 8. RED RIVER VALLEY (MINN. AND N.D.-MAN.)-
-HISTORY--19TH CENTURY. 9. UNITED NORWEGIAN LUTHERAN
CHURCH OF AMERICA--CLERGY--BIOGRAPHY. I. KILDAHL, ERLING
E., 1917- II. TITLE.
  F615.S2K55 2008
  977.6'04092--DC22
  [B]
                                    2007051808

CONTENTS

ACKNOWLEDGEMENTS

In the task of revising and editing my father's manuscript, I have been aided by a number of persons who furnished answers to questions and puzzles that arose. My sister, Mrs. Nicoline Clara Kildahl Shalda, wrote many letters to me answering and amplifying details of queries I had posed. She was my oldest surviving sibling, was keenly interested in these memoirs, had created a novel based upon them, and had worked closely with my father when he was writing or dictating his remembrances. Unfortunately, her long life (1901-1990) recently ended, and although I cannot thank her in person, I do so here in her memory.

My Aunt, Nilsine Johanna Kildahl, (1867-1967) the author's young sister, published, in 1949 in The Lutheran Herald, a two part reminiscence of the family's life in Urland Valley, Goodhue County, Minnesota. She also wrote informative letters to my sister Clara, who turned them over to me. I am grateful for her help.

I am indebted to: Beverly Voldseth Allers, Director (in 1986) and Caroline M. de Mauriac, Executive Director (in 1989) of Northfield Historical Society, for the correction of details and facts included in my father's description of the infamous James-Younger gang's attempted holdup of the Northfield Bank in September, 1876; Mr. Gordon Cowan of Churchs Ferry, North Dakota, who graciously and generously shared with me his knowledge and records of dry lakes and land holdings in the Maza and Churchs Ferry areas; the manager of Crossroads Restaurant, located near Churchs Ferry, who unerringly guided me to Antiochia Church and its graveyard where my paternal grandparents, as well as an uncle, are buried; and Orville Olson, Curator, Goodhue County Historical Society, for invaluable help in location of sites and the history of Goodhue County. To all, my heartfelt thanks.

Last, I wish to express special gratitude to my late wife, Maxine Kildahl, for her steadfast encouragement and love as well as her comments, suggestions, and corrections during this endeavor.

PREFACE

ERLING E. KILDAHL

During my father's lifetime, nothing was done with his manuscript other than putting it in typewritten form. No attempt was made to edit, arrange, revise, or in any way prepare it for possible publication. After his death in 1945, my sister, Nicoline Clara Kildahl Shalda, who had helped Father by typing his scribblings and jottings, took charge of the memoirs. She wrote a novel based on them which, unfortunately, never found a publisher.

In the 1960s and 70s, I became, probably by default, but also because I had always been interested in our roots, the unofficial family archivist. All kinds of material, including photographs, letters, documents, and this manuscript came into my hands. After I read it, I put it away with other material but made a vow to work on it "sometime" in the vague future, when I had time or when I retired from my professorship at Purdue University. Its presence, however, kept nagging at me. Something had to be done with it; my father's story must be given a chance to reach print and readers.

Rephrasing, rewriting, and reorganization has been necessary to give the original writing clarity and cohesion. The manuscript is replete with jottings, unfinished and incomplete phrases and sentences, and misplaced paragraphs. The basic story, tone, and intention, I trust, have been preserved. The purpose of all revisions and editing is to make the memoirs as readable and enjoyable as possible.

I have omitted some material on family history in Norway. This is the story of Harold B. Kildahl Sr., his parents, and his siblings, in America. We begin, then, with the family preparing to emigrate, shortly before their actual embarkation for America.

INTRODUCTION

Harold Berg Kildahl Sr., who found time in his busy life to dictate or hastily scribble remembrances of his youth and early manhood, became more and more aware as the years passed, that he had lived through, had, indeed, participated in, an unique transitional period of America's history.

The Civil War had ended just a year before he and his family arrived from Norway. The people of the United States were turning away from preoccupation with civil strife and dissension to peaceful opportunities and new horizons. Much of the country west of the Mississippi River was open, untamed, and unsettled. An abundance of free land was available to anyone for the taking, thanks to the Homestead Act of 1862. The promise of free, fertile, and probably flat land was an irresistible attraction to immigrants from mountainous Norway. In the 1860s and 70s Norwegians emigrated to North America by the hundreds as later they came by the thousands.

Coming to America meant more than escape from poor soil, small farms, and absence of opportunity in rural Norway—it meant (although many may have only dimly realized it, if at all) embracing new concepts of life, heightening ambitions and achievements, and reaching goals theretofore only dreamt of in Scandinavia. The great migration from Europe in the nineteenth century is taken for granted today, but we can have nothing but admiration for those brave souls who sold their holdings, pulled up their roots, and risked all on the chance for a new life in a strange land.

The Kildahl family lived on a farm called Hundseth, located in a region named Namdalseidet, west of Trondhjem Fjord, in western Norway. A combination of unproductive soil and seven consecutive years of early fall frosts helped my father's parents to decide to emigrate. They sold Hundseth and, after satisfying all financial obligations, had just enough money remaining to pay their fares to Chicago. Fortunately, it was a sizable sum because there were a lot of fares to be paid. The family consisted of father Johan, mother Nicoline Buvarp, and their children: Anna Delise, 19; Nils, 16; Pauline Mathilde, (hereinafter Matilda) 14; Andrew J., 12; John Nathan, (hereinafter Nathan or J. N.) 9; Johanna, 3½; and Harold Berg, my father, 1 year old.

During his childhood and youth, Father lived in hillside dugouts and prairie shanties, drove or walked oxen teams and saw the last of the Red River ox cart trains, rode on steamboats, saw railroads laid down and boom towns spring up, die, or move (lock, stock, and keg) to follow the westering rails, lived in Northfield when the James-Younger gang attempted to rob the First National Bank and participated in the excitement that that event engendered, witnessed cattle drives arriving at railheads and a town "hoorawed," terrorized, by wildly riding, recklessly shooting, drunken cowboys, knew of claim jumpers unceremoniously lynched by angry citizens, witnessed and helped fight prairie fires that swept unhindered for miles, collected bison horns and bones to sell and chips to use as fuel, plowed virgin prairie soil thick with buffalo grass in Dakota Territory, participated in a land filing rush—in short, was part of much that now, nostalgically, is thought of as the lore and romance of the West, celebrated endlessly in all media and which has become a permanent part of the American psyche.

My father was aware that his siblings and he embodied, in microcosm, the three principal interests of late nineteenth century immigrants in rural America: one, to secure land, develop it, establish farms, and sink roots; two, to gain coveted education and fulfill personal ambitions; and three, to follow the lure of the frontier as it marched westward. Three of Father's brothers and sisters sought the first goal; three, including the author, wanted education and a different kind of life; and one caught the frontier fever, ran away from home, and became a cowboy with The American Cattle Company—no farming or formal education for him. Out of touch for years, and the cause of much worry to his parents, he eventually bobbed up and later became a rancher near Miles City,

Montana. Thus, in one family of the time, was manifested three strong forces motivating the people of America.

The author realized his ambition to acquire an education and enter the ministry. After five years of successful farming near Maza, Dakota Territory, he set off, at age 23, in pursuit of his dream. In the course of a decade he regained lost ground at the elementary and secondary school levels, went on to and was graduated from the recently established St. Olaf College (of the United Norwegian Lutheran Church, organized in 1890) in Northfield, Minnesota, and then completed his training for the ministry at the Lutheran seminary in Minneapolis. Starting almost from scratch, in that brief span of time, he became an ordained pastor in the Lutheran Church in 1898.

Harold B. Kildahl Sr. wrote his remembrances in the 1920s and early 1930s. They were meant, primarily, for the eyes of his children and grandchildren "that they should know whence they came." His memoirs have an appeal for a much wider audience, I believe, despite the fact that the story related here has, in general terms, been described elsewhere in both historical and fictional form. The work of others, though, cannot detract from the immediacy of his impressions and the impact of his eyewitness accounts of events he encountered during his early life.

Again, the reader is reminded that the body of work that follows is in my father's words. All footnotes and emendations, however, have been added by me, Erling E. Kildahl

Harold B. Kildahl, Sr.

I

IN TRANSIT

Hundseth Farm, Namdalseidet, Norway.
Harold B. Kildahl's birthplace.

1

IRREVOCABLE DECISION

In my parents' decision to emigrate, as in many of life's endeavors and enterprises, it is the young people who have the vision and energy to get things moving. My oldest brother, Nils, in particular, led the way in persuading my parents to sell the farm and move the family to America. I never got to know him but from all accounts he was an unusually bright and energetic young man. By the time he was sixteen he had written an English grammar and a Norwegian-English lexicon, and had read everything he could find on conditions in America. He was ambitious and optimistic and could see no bright future for himself or the family in Norway. Canny, he won Mother as an eager ally and the two of them soon persuaded my reluctant father to agree to the move. The farm, Hundseth, was put up for sale and, largely at Nils's urging, Redwing, in the state of Minnesota, was to be our destination. Why Redwing was selected I do not know, but other Norwegians had found a new life there and that may have been good enough reason to make the Mississippi river settlement our immediate goal in the New World.

It was not a casual matter to make the difficult decision and then prepare a large family to sail to America in those days. It meant leaving dear friends and relatives behind, perhaps never to see them again, and the voyage itself would present unforeseen troubles. The ship we were to board did not provide food for its passengers; each family or individual had to furnish and store enough provisions to last ten weeks. Our family of nine would subsist on flat bread, potatoes, dried beef, bologna, salt pork, salt fish, and cheese for that length of time. We would also need enough clean clothes to last the length of the trip because there would be no laundry (or bathing) facilities on the ship, not a happy prospect to contemplate.

Passage had been procured on the three-masted sailing ship Nicanor, Captain Morck commanding. The *Nicanor* was due to sail May 25th, 1866, from Trondhjem and all passengers were notified to be aboard by the 24th, which meant my family had to leave the farm on Monday, May 14th. In the midst of preparations for departure, tragedy struck. On May 12th, lovely 3½ year old Johanna died of scarlet fever. That sudden, almost insupportable calamity nearly destroyed the fabric of our family, my mother told me when I was older, and would have caused the cancellation of the trip if that had been possible. In deep grief, my parents made arrangements with Uncle Daniel Kaldahl, one of Father's brothers,[1] who owned a neighboring farm, to attend to her funeral while they tore themselves away in order to reach the ship on time. They never got over the heartrending necessity of leaving Johanna unburied and unknelled in Norway, unable to attend her funeral or properly mourn her untimely death.

On the 14th, the family, forced to put misfortune behind them, were driven in a wagon to Fosnesstranden at the great bend of Trondhjem Fjord. There we boarded the steamboat *Indhered* and, with fair weather prevailing, arrived in Trondhjem the evening of the same day. It was just as well we had reached the city a little early because all passengers scheduled for the Nicanor were required to have a medical examination before they were permitted to board and the examinations took considerable time to complete. While waiting for the 24th and embarkation, the 17th of May, Norway's Independence Day, was celebrated with parades, music, and speeches which helped my parents, brothers, and sisters get their minds away from mournful thoughts of Johanna.

2

TRANSATLANTIC PASSAGE

Finally the great day arrived and my family found suitable quarters on board the ship, located a safe place to stow their possessions and their precious, irreplaceable food that had to last the entire trip. Many years later I met and talked with Mr. J. E. Jorgenson who, as a 6½ year old child, was a fellow passenger on that voyage. He and my brother Nathan became playmates during the trip, but lost touch with each other in America. He told me the *Nicanor* was an old salt freighter that had been remodelled for transporting emigrants, thus meeting a growing demand for low cost passage across the Atlantic. There were about 300 passengers aboard, he told me, but didn't remember whether the ship was over-crowded or not.

Mr. Jorgenson did recall there were several rows of bunks made of rough lumber built into the ship. Each bunk was furnished with a straw tick but passengers were required to furnish their own bedding. There were no private cabins, not even partitions separating the rows of bunks, but there were dividers between the ends of them. He told me the passengers kept their luggage under or beside their beds, but he did not remember how many decks were outfitted with these bunks. There did not seem to be any embarrassment about getting into or out of bed because the passengers all wore heavy woolen underwear and slept in it. He confirmed to me that there were no bathing facilities but there were bathrooms of a sort where passengers could wash their hands and faces and take care of bodily needs.

Mr. Jorgenson told me there was no furniture; passengers had to sit on their bunks, trunks, or chests but there were some large stoves on the deck where the passengers could do light cooking such as making coffee (which few could afford) or soup. He remembered that his father had brought a keg of buttermilk and another of homemade beer but that both turned so sour before his family had consumed them that they became undrinkable and had to be thrown overboard. He told me, too, that ventilation below decks was poor and passengers who were not seasick spent their time on deck if weather permitted. I am fortunate that Mr. Jorgenson and I met and that he graciously shared his memories of the *Nicanor* and the voyage with me. I was barely one year old when we emigrated and, of course, have no recollection of the event, and, strangely enough, little was said about it in our family while I was growing up.

On sailing day, May 25th, religious services were conducted on the main deck which was crowded with passengers, visitors, and crew. On the stroke of 6:00 P.M., the docking cables were let go and the steam tug *Finmarken* took the *Nicanor* in tow to guide it through the fjord out to the Norwegian Sea, a reach of the Atlantic Ocean. According to my father's daily notations of the trip, a count of the passengers was taken on the 26th to discover anyone on board without a ticket. If such a person was found he or she would be sent back with the pilot when the ship cleared Trondhjem Fjord. No illegal passengers were discovered and the pilot left us at the mouth of the fjord.

Upon clearing land, the *Nicanor* immediately encountered a severe storm driving down from the northwest. After four full days of strong winds and high seas, the ship, loaded with seasick voyagers, found itself only sixty miles from Scotland's rugged coast as the storm subsided. The original course was resumed and everyone enjoyed a few days of normal weather and winds for that time of year in the North Atlantic, but on Sunday, June 3rd, the *Nicanor* passed south of the Faroe Islands in heavy fog. Despite the weather conditions, the passengers desired religious services and, in the absence of an ordained pastor, my father volunteered to conduct them. Evidently he satisfied the others because this was a duty he undertook each subsequent Sunday of the voyage.

During the next two weeks the *Nicanor* made good speed, favored by steady winds, and during that time no untoward incident occurred that Father's notations indicate.

On June 16th we neared the Newfoundland Banks, sailing into much colder weather caused by huge icebergs in the area. On that day, too, Nils, the hope and mainstay of my family, became ill. Medical facilities on board were minimal, I understand, but there was a ship's doctor attending him who did everything he could for my brother. His condition steadily worsened until the early morning of June 21st when he died of what was then called brain fever. Captain Morck conducted his funeral, held the same day, and Nils's body, wrapped in a sail and weighted with bags of sand, was consigned to the cold ocean depths.

The sudden, unexpected loss of the oldest son and brother devastated my family, my parents especially. Nils's death nearly destroyed my mother who was unable, she later told me, to leave her bunk. It seemed to her that darkness surrounded her and all seemed lost because Nils was the family leader upon whom she depended. He was the driving force behind the move to America; he had learned English so as to be the family guide in the new land; he had made the preparations, chosen the destination, had created and maintained the family's enthusiasm for the migration by his vision of a new and different life abroad—and now he was no more. Years later she said that in the days following his death she nearly lost her mind and wouldn't have cared if the ship had gone down.

Father wrote in his diary:

> Nils's death was a great loss and caused us profound sorrow. He was sixteen and a half years old, Johanna was three and a half and now both died within thirty nine days of each other. It was God's will. The Lord gave, the Lord has taken away, blessed be the name of the Lord!

It was this deep faith that sustained my parents in their desolation. They realized they must go on and try to fulfill Nils's hopes and plans for the family in the new world. They would miss him dearly in the days ahead, but they were determined to follow through to the best of their abilities without his command of English and his intelligent guidance. In time, my parents added two more children to the family and, in honor of Johanna and Nils, gave the babies the same names, thus perpetuating the dead children's memories in new life in a new land.

On June 27th, the *Nicanor* was in the midst of the Grand Banks, which are east and southeast of Newfoundland where fish abounded and some of the passengers cast lines with great success, I'm told, making a welcome addition to their seemingly endless dried and salted food diet. Finally, on July 1st, the ship went through Cabot Strait into the Gulf of St. Lawrence. The weather was clear and most passengers, my father recorded in his notations, were on deck although there was little more than water to see. During the next few days the favorable winds drove the ship across the gulf, and into the St. Lawrence River. On July 6th, only, forty miles from Quebec City, a pilot came on board and took charge of the *Nicanor.*

On July 9th, after 44 days at sea, we disembarked on Grosse Island where, during that day and part of the next, everyone of board was examined by a Provincial doctor. Shortly after noon of the second day, we were declared fit and were cleared to proceed to the city where we arrived at 4:00 P.M., July 10th, six weeks and four days after leaving Trondhjem.

3

REDWING OR BUST

The *Nicanor* remained docked at Quebec City for three days, then proceeded up-river to Montreal where it arrived at 1:00 P.M. on July 14th. The next day, on terra firma after the long voyage, the family went sightseeing. The storied French-Canadian city, with clean, paved streets and well designed buildings, especially the Gothic Church of Notre Dame, made a strong impression on my parents. The family attended mass in the great church in thanksgiving for their safe arrival in North America despite the fact we were of the Lutheran faith and the service, in Latin, was strange to them. On July 16th the baggage of the migrating families was transferred to the steamboat *Spartan*, but before my family left the *Nicanor*, Captain Morck, who was later remembered as a most impressive man, bade us goodbye and presented Father a photograph of himself, a memento of the trip from Norway my parents prized and kept as long as they lived.

The next day the *Spartan*, after traveling up-river all night entered Lake Ontario and on the 18th the steamer landed at Hamilton, Ontario, where the emigrant families and their belongings were transferred to a waiting train made up of cattle cars. A vigorous protest was lodged, through interpreters, against such shabby treatment with the result some old and rickety passenger cars were substituted for the freight cars. Reluctantly, the group of travelers entrained for the trip to Detroit.

That attempt to fob off cattle cars on immigrants when passenger cars were expected and paid for was only the first of a number of attempts to hoodwink the unsuspecting innocents from abroad. At first they were easy marks for cheats and tricksters, but they soon caught on to such confidence games. The next day, my family's grievances against the railroad diminished when, in the United States at last, we encountered our first example of American "enterprise." Two slickers told the newcomers it would cost $1.00 per family to proceed on their way. Some of the families paid before they realized they were being duped, and none was prevented from boarding another train that would take them to Chicago. Those who paid did not get their money back—the tricksters had disappeared. Upon arrival in Chicago, the group that had come on such a long journey together separated, amid tears and friendly farewells, to go on to their respective destinations.

In 1866 Chicago was a sprawling, rapidly growing center of railroads, manufacturing, and commerce of all kinds. My family arrived in this bustling city practically penniless. The rail fare from Montreal to the Windy City, $9.00 per person, plus expenditures for food, had almost exhausted the family's funds. Now alone, no longer one of a group of families who had helped each other, we had to consult our own resources to find a way to continue on to Redwing. Evidently no serious consideration was given to changing our destination. Nils had chosen, planned, and prepared for our reception there and Redwing remained the family's goal. My parents had to find funds, somehow, to enable us to reach the Minnesota settlement, but their first attempt to do so ended in sorry disillusionment.

Father had a married niece, living in Chicago, who had made her home with us for two years in Norway. My parents had not only cared for her at Hundseth, but had nursed her through a long and harrowing illness, for which she had expressed her undying gratitude. Feeling close kinship, they had no qualms in turning to her in their difficulty, confident she would be only too happy to help them get to Minnesota. But then, when it came to the crunch, so to speak, she was found wanting. Not only would she not aid us, but informed my parents that she did not care to have anything to do with us. She did, however, relent enough to permit my mother to wash the family's clothes in her basement. This disappointing encounter with our ungrateful relative did have one beneficial result: it taught a powerful lesson in the ways of the world, at least in Chicago. It is to my parents' credit that they did not allow the niece's despicable behavior to sour them in their relationships that were to come. They kept their faith in the goodness of people and seldom, if ever, allowed cynicism to color their thoughts, words, or behavior. I am proud that they remained open, frank, and trusting till the end of their long lives. However, they never saw or corresponded with the niece again.

Our family remained four days in Chicago sheltered in immigrant quarters near a railroad depot. Everybody in the family was travel weary and needed a rest but the worry of money hung over us. Funds had to be found somehow and they were, but at a sacrifice. Father, ever the scholar and book lover, had brought favorite volumes, his only assets, with him to America. As his last resort, as much as he hated to do it, he sold them to a Norwegian book store owner named O. T. Relling, who gave him a fair price.

The sale of the books raised enough money to pay the family's rail and steamboat fares to Redwing, but there would be stopovers along the way. On July 25th, at 11:00 P.M., we arrived in Stoughton, Wisconsin, and soon encountered big trouble.

I quote from Father's diary:

> We arrived in Stoughton late and were told that we could not spend the night in the depot. The agent waved us out, locked the door, and left. We arranged ourselves to stay on the depot platform during the night. About one in the morning three men came along who acted very insultingly towards the women who began to cry for help, which woke me. I tried to protect the women, but was knocked down by one of the men so that I saw stars and was not able to rise to my feet for some time, but we all yelled for help as loud as we could and the ruffians fled.

After that experience, the family, in council, decided it would be best to get away from the railroad station. One of my brothers saw a light in a building up the street and, gathering our possessions, the family walked toward the structure which turned out to be a hotel. My parents tried to tell the clerk about their experiences on the depot platform, but could not make themselves understood nor could they grasp his words except one, "money." When the night clerk understood they had none, he opened the door and ushered us back into the dark. With no place to turn, my family spread blankets on the sidewalk and slept the rest of the night under a store awning. (In the 1920s I often visited Stoughton in the course of my work. I looked for that store which, in a way, had sheltered my family, but never found it. Many years had passed since our adventure and the store was no longer in existence.) Father, discouraged by misfortunes and reluctant to go farther on the way to Redwing, even though the fare was paid, sought work as a teacher in Stoughton, a Norwegian population center, but there was no vacancy available.

Father's search for employment delayed our continuing journey but a few days later we arrived in Prairie du Chien, Wisconsin, again late in the evening. A resident, who spoke Norwegian, told my parents that there was no railroad station where my family could stay the night and offered to lodge us all for $5.00, an amount we could not afford. The Norwegian-speaking cheat warned my folks that we would have to sleep on the sidewalk, but another, kinder, Swedish-speaking stranger interrupted the former's lie and told my family that there was a train depot where we could spend the night. Following the latter's directions, we found the station, spread our bedding on the floor, spent a comfortable night, and saved five precious dollars. As I indicated earlier, immigrants were considered easy marks by confidence men, even those who were recently-arrived newcomers themselves who had no qualms about cheating their own kind.

II

MINNESOTA

Harold B. Kildahl, Age 15.

4

DESTINATION

At 8:00 A.M. on the morning of August 8th, my family boarded a steamboat for the trip up the Mississippi River to Redwing, where we disembarked about 3:00 P.M. the same day. We had arrived at the ultimate destination envisioned by my dead brother, Nils, so long before. His plans had come to fruition exactly 75 days after the *Nicanor* weighed anchor in Trondhjem harbor. It had been a difficult, heart-wrenching, period of time for the entire family, those two and a half months, but my father's diary makes no particular note of the occasion. He merely indicates that we were welcomed at the dock by a Swedish resident who took us to his home and treated us cordially, who introduced us to our new world quite properly, but Father did not record the greeter's name. I assume the latter's presence at the steamboat landing had been arranged by Nils in his pre-trip planning.

Father wrote in his diary:

> It so happened that Rev. B. J. Muus[2] came to Redwing to conduct a service that evening in the auditorium of the County Court House. We attended this service and were delighted to hear a Lutheran sermon in our own language.

At the conclusion of the service, according to the diary:

Rev. Muus kindly took my wife and our youngest child, Harold, with him in his buggy to his parsonage. He also arranged with a farmer named Henrik Evensen to take the other children and me to the Follingstads, a farm family who lived five miles from the parsonage. The Follingstads received us very kindly and provided lodgings for us for the night.

All that generous and considerate treatment of us by Pastor Muus and his friends contrasted sharply with the behavior of others encountered in America. Mother told me later that during the buggy ride with the pastor and me she felt quite special and flattered, just the tonic she needed after the ordeal of the long trip from Norway. She enjoyed and appreciated the solicitude and kindness given us by those friendly strangers, but both she and my father realized the warmth shown them sprang fully from Pastor Muus's tremendous influence and prestige among the Norwegian settlers in that part of the state.

The next day my father walked the five miles to the parsonage. Rev. Muus offered to let him take a wagon, a pair of oxen, and a driver to Follingstad's farm to fetch the other children and our baggage to the pastor's home where we all remained until August 13th. Again aided by the pastor, my family found shelter with the family of Nils Kvernodden, who lived on a farm about a mile and a half from the parsonage. The Kvernoddens had a small log house on their land that was available for our use, and, I was later told, my family was very happy to have a house, small as it was, all to themselves. Privacy was a luxury to be fully enjoyed, at least for a while, after the long and tedious journey from Norway.

My father's diary and notations of the trip to America and arrival in Goodhue County end at this point. Brief and cryptic as his notes are, they have proved invaluable to me in the preparation of these memoirs. Hereinafter, I [Harold B. Kildahl, Sr., the author] am indebted to many different sources, chiefly the reminiscences of my parents, siblings, and friends from our early days in America, and my own memories.[3]

Pastor Muus, a strong supporter of education on all levels, needed a teacher to serve his many congregations in Goodhue and adjacent counties. He immediately engaged Father to teach religious school on a circuit basis, which meant he would conduct a class for one week in one farm house, then move to another for a week, and so on around the circuit of congregations. Goodhue County was still, in 1866, pioneer territory despite the admission of Minnesota to the union in 1858. The county lacked schools and churches and settlers were still living in one-room log cabins. Classes conducted by my father had to be held in that one room which caused, no doubt, great inconvenience to the owner-residents. Father, in a catch-as-catch-can situation, often slept in low lofts and sheds and occasionally found a snow drift on his bed in the morning. His always dubious health was not improved by those conditions, but, in the family's circumstances, he was happy to have found work and an income.

Weaving was a skill learned by my mother as a child and she became proficient at the loom. When Mrs. Muus became aware of Mother's competence, she engaged her services, procured a loom, and set her to work making blankets, carpets, and other products. (When we were big enough, my young sister Nilsine Johanna and I helped her by sewing rags, a pound a day each, to be used in carpet making.) The pastor's wife also hired Anna, my oldest sister, to work in the parsonage. With three incomes my family gradually began to gain financial independence. During the next two years the Muus family befriended and aided mine, kindnesses extended in a time of great need, never forgotten by my parents.

One particular intervention by Rev. Muus in our affairs is memorable and greatly appreciated by me. Often immigrants were induced to change their sometimes difficult Norwegian surnames to something more convenient for American English pronunciation. Thus we have many Norwegian-American families named Johnson, Olson, Anderson, Nelson, etc. Efforts were made by some in the community to have us change our name to Johnson, but when Rev. Muus heard of those suggestions, he conferred with my parents, who, at his urging, I'm sure, decided against the change. Americans we encountered would just have to get used to the name Kildahl and do some adapting of their own. To the time of this writing, (1926) the name has not caused any particular hardship to my non-Scandinavian friends.

5

DUGOUT HOMES AND
RATTLESNAKES

My family was eager to settle on a farm as soon as possible and my parents talked with Rev. Muus about their desires to own their own place. But before that goal could be achieved, an addition to the family occurred. About a year after our arrival in Goodhue County, on September 3rd, 1867, the most important date thus far in our life in America, a baby girl was born. She was given the names Nilsine Johanna, in honor of both of our recently deceased siblings, Nils and Johanna, and was baptized by Rev. Muus.

During the following year, as we were all adjusting to the presence of the new family member, and my parents could concentrate on other matters, Rev. Muus told them he had discovered a forty-acre plot of railroad land that was available for purchase. It was located about six miles from the parsonage, in the Urland Valley, near the town of Leon,[4] Goodhue County, and could be bought for a reasonable price on favorable terms. The Pastor helped my family procure that land, which, although hilly and thickly timbered in part, offered good soil and, gushing from a hillside, a fine spring that would furnish all the water we would need. The lower part of the land parcel flattened out into a lush meadow which extended down to the stream that ran through the valley. The stream was found to be well stocked with fish, a welcome addition to the family's diet.

After the land was acquired by my parents and a rudimentary dugout home was made near the spring, livestock, particularly a cow, became an urgent need. Again Rev. Muus came to my family's aid. He arranged with one of his congregants to sell us a cow on easy terms, which led to the construction of a log stable to house the animal and store the hay-like grass that grew wild in the meadow. Before the cow could eat the hay in the luxury of her new home, the boys of the family had a lot of work to do. First, prepare some long poles, then cut the tall grass with sickles, lay the grass on a pair of poles, and use them to carry the hay to the barn.

All that activity and progress made my mother cheerful and happy, she told me when I was older. She felt that prosperity was smiling upon us in our adopted country. She was strong and healthy and, with the help of my older brothers Andrew and Nathan, cleared and cultivated some of the land. In addition to that hard, heavy labor, she found time and energy to do some weaving and also to care for my baby sister and me. In the meantime, Father continued with his salaried school work, earning income that paid for the cow as well as installment payments on the land.

On April 4th, 1869, my oldest sister, Anna Delise, was married to Mr. Ole P. Jermstad, and settled near Glenwood, Minnesota. After they arrived and settled into their new surroundings, they wrote my parents a letter describing, in glowing terms, the conditions that prevailed in their community, a situation that would be a marked improvement over our present circumstances. They wrote that my parents could easily obtain 160 acres of level land with lakeshore, timber, and large clearings. That glittering prospect induced my parents to sell their land in Goodhue County and arrangements were made with their new son-in-law to transport us, our cow, and our furniture to Pope County on the day the dugout was vacated. Ole Jermstad, a reliable man, had agreed to the arrangement, and had, with my parents permission, even selected our new home for us.

The farm in Goodhue County had been sold to Mr. and Mrs. Meraker, the day was set for our move, and Ole planned to come for us. Anticipation ran high in the family and everyone was eager to get started for our new home, when disaster struck down our hopes. Father came home from a week of school work and complained of being ill. His condition continually worsened until he had to take to his bed. Ole and Anna were informed of this development and the move to Pope County was postponed. The day soon came for the new owners to take possession of the farm. The Merakers had given up their former quarters and needed to move into the dugout, which, of course, they had every right to do. They helped us move our things out—not too carefully; one item of furniture was smashed and other pieces marred, much to my mother's dismay, but worse, we now had no place to call our own and were forced to camp in the open.

One incident involving Mrs. Meraker has, ever since I was told of it, remained in my memory, gladdened my heart, and strengthened my belief in the law of compensation. There was a short, deep, side-valley, or gully nearby which was called Rattlesnake Valley because it was home to a large number of the creatures. Mother warned Mrs. Meraker of the danger but she declared she was not afraid of rattlers no matter how many there were. We were camped some distance away from both the Merakers and the snakes but one day loud and repeated screams were heard coming from the valley of the snakes. Mr. Meraker, who came to investigate the disturbance, found his wife standing on a large, flat boulder. Every time she tried to step off the rock, a rattler would poke his head out until she was surrounded, and began screaming. After she was rescued, her husband and their sons killed a great number of those snakes that had their nests under that stone. Mrs. Meraker never again boasted of her fearlessness; the reptiles obviously had gained her respect. I was too young to remember the incident, but I'm sure my siblings and parents had a laugh or two at Mrs. Meraker's expense.

A neighbor named Amund Meland, seeing my family's plight, very generously took us into his two-room log cabin home. The move from our camp was only a half mile but during that event my first memory was formed, a memory intimately associated with grief and tears. How much better, I've often thought, if my first remembrance had been a happy, joyful one. To move my father to the cabin, a bed was made up for him in a wagon because he was not able to sit up in the spring seat, and my new sister shared the bed with him. I did not like the arrangement. I wanted to ride too but there was no room for me and I, disconsolate, cried as if my heart was broken as the wagon moved away without me. It seems to me yet that there might have been a tiny corner for me. Mother gave me a little basket with two or three potatoes in it and, to comfort me, told me she depended on her little man to help her carry food to the cabin. It helped, and I stopped crying.

When we were about half way up the valley we had to cross a stream on a fallen log that served as a footbridge. Mother sat down on the end of that log, took me in her lap, hugged me to her, and sobbed, her body shaking violently. I put my arms around her neck and she soon regained her composure. My trouble had been minor, merely wounded pride, I realize now, but she was truly the one in need of comfort and cheer with a husband sick in bed, a family of small children, no home of her own, and nothing to depend upon for income. How could we go on living? The situation, she later told me, seemed hopeless. But she was a tough-minded woman, my mother! Inner strength made her gather herself together and, hugging and kissing me, and drying our tears, we proceeded up the valley.

That surely was a time when all of Mother's strength, character, and faith were tapped to sustain her and her family. It was the first but not the last time I sympathized with her. Despite grievous troubles, of which we seemed to have plenty, she was always thoughtful and considerate of her children. I know there were times when she fed us and had only peelings and scraps for herself. She truly possessed seemingly limitless reserves of courage and resourcefulness. It was not for nothing neighbors, relatives, and friends in Norway had called her "Underbarnet," (the wonder child) when, in her early teens, she was her father's right hand. Her breakdown on the log bridge was one of the few times in her life that she acknowledged an obstacle in the path of what she wanted to accomplish. But not for long; she found a way around that hindrance, too. During that short walk from the old to the new home, she experienced a spiritual renewal and by the time we arrived at Mr. Meland's log cabin she was herself again.

6

NEW HOME, NEW FRIENDS, NEW LIFE

Our second home consisted of an excavation about seven feet deep into the side of a steep hill with the jutting front and sides constructed of logs, with a half window on each side of the door in the front wall. The roof of the log portion was made of straw and sod laid on stringers. It was sited on the north side of a deep, narrow gully just below the junction of two valleys. In the spring of the year or after heavy rains, streams formed in these valleys which, joined, became a torrent running past our home. I enjoyed playing in those streams, innocently taking great risks, and I am lucky I didn't drown.

Upon entering our single room combination dwelling, a visitor would see, in the left front corner of the room near a window, the loom Mother used to weave rag carpets and blankets for customers. In the other front corner was the stove with a stove pipe running up and through the roof. Next to the stove along the right wall was a cupboard and in the rear corner on that side was a double-deck bed with Father in the lower deck. Opposite, in the left rear corner, was another double-deck bed for the children. In the middle of the room was a post supporting the roof beam that extended from the front gable to the rear of the room. Nailed to the post was a shelf on which Mother kept a tin plate containing grease and a wick, the only source of artificial light in our home. A large emigrant chest with a flat top, in the middle of the room just in front of the center post, served as a table. Three benches, hewed from logs, completed the furnishings with the exception of a pretty little footstool, which I loved. The floor was wood.

For a few years there was quite a colony of dugout homes in those valleys. Immigrants came and dug themselves in until they could afford another move toward the frontier where land could be had for the taking. In a more or less regular progression, the dugout families came and went; we greeted them and bade them good-bye, hoping always we could soon follow, but Father's illness kept us there year after year, frustrating Mother's ambition to own a good piece of land where she knew she could do well.

Our home was located in the midst of dense forest. Little Nilsine Johanna, two and a half years my junior, was my only playmate. We waded the streams and roamed among the magnificent trees, or played with wood chips and pebbles, our only toys made wondrous through imagination. The trees were our friends, we gave many of them names, and grieved when the owner of the land cut down some of our biggest and most beloved companions. Attached to nature since those days, I still find my most enjoyable recreation in roaming the woods and communing with my old friends. If tree surgery had been known and taught when I was young, I think my ambition to be a pastor would have been a forlorn hope. All my majestic friends are, or soon will be, gone, destroyed by man's insatiable need for lumber and other wood products. I am happy I lived in a time when they were still abundant, for there is no sight like a stand of virgin timber, each tree huge and hundreds of years old. Once gone, I fear we shall never see their like again.

My young sister never lost her love for, or was long out of touch with, our forest friends, either, and went on in her life to study them and other of nature's creatures and wonders. Later, when time became available to her, she earned her degree in Biology in 1898 and her Master's degree in the same subject in 1900 from the University of North Dakota, supporting herself as an assistant in that department. In 1901, then Instructor of Biology, she began summer study at the University of Chicago in Botany. In 1905 she was offered and accepted a scholarship in botanical studies. Ultimately, she earned her Ph.D. there in Botany in 1909, a culmination of her abiding love for the silent, giant forest friends of our childhood. She put her knowledge to good use, not only as a teacher of Botany but as an appointed member of a national commission charged with exploring and cataloguing the flora of the

Territory of Alaska, interest in which had been re-awakened by the Gold Rush of 1898. She spent considerable time in Alaska and, despite the hardships she encountered, did commendable work for the Federal government. Unfortunately, the beginning of a singular career was curtailed by family circumstances.

Mr. Meland, the owner of the forest land surrounding our home, permitted my family to cut dead and downed branches and trees for fuel which was transported to the house during the winter on a large handsled. My brothers generally cut wood found up-hill from the dugout, thus minimizing their transportation problems, but it made little difference to Josie or me where they found it because we enjoyed playing "horses" during the hauling, turning work into play. Our water supply came from a small spring a little farther down the valley but it occasionally dried up, forcing us then to go to a more distant spring. It was a matter for rejoicing when water reappeared in the nearer spring, incidently Kildahl means spring valley.

Putting food on the table was always a pressing problem, my mother later told me. Anna was married and gone and the remaining older children were working for their keep. In 1868, sixteen year old Matilda had gone as a maid for a family in Minneapolis and Andrew, when he turned fifteen in 1869, became apprentice to a carpenter. Remaining at home after Andrew's departure were Nilsine Johanna, Nathan, and I, who had to be fed and clothed, responsibilities that devolved upon my mother.

To ease the burden, a comparatively wealthy man in the community offered to adopt Nathan and give him his name, a fairly common occurrence of that era. My parents considered the proposal but after talking with Nathan about the offer the decision was made to turn it down. We remained in poverty but we were in it together. Mother, seeking ways to keep the larder full, learned basket weaving, in addition to her other skills, and since there was a fairly brisk market for them, managed to add quite a bit to our money supply. She made them of basswood bark or willow and Nathan and I helped by delivering them to purchasers in the neighborhood. (I visited Urland Valley a few years ago and an old man presented me with a basket he had bought from Mother when we lived there. I prize that touching gift.)[5] Mother also sewed work shirts, overalls, and comfortable cloth shoes called "labba," which we also sold to neighbors. In harvest time she was hired by nearby farmers to clean up after the threshers were done. That work enabled her to gather enough wheat to provide our family with flour for a year, as well as middlings[6] and bran for the cow and pig we had acquired. Somehow, means were found to keep food on the table and fuel in the stove, but little could be saved for a future move to a real farm.

Washtado, a post office and country store, was located about two miles from our home.[7] The postmaster and proprietor of the store, a Mr. Thompson, who was a kind man, always gave us children a piece of candy, a rare treat, whenever we visited the store. I was especially thankful to him one day when I was to have a new pair of leather shoes in place of my "labba." None fit, so he brought out a pair of boots, the finest I have ever seen, with brass toes and red leather decoration. Although they cost twenty five cents more than shoes, I wanted them, and hoped they would fit. They did! I looked at Mother, hoping she would buy them for me. With a little smile, looking at me, she found the money and paid. That was one of the happiest days of my childhood.

On September 30th, 1871, Nils was born. He was given the name of our eldest brother who died at sea off the Newfoundland Banks. From that time on, Nilsine Johanna became simply Johanna, (hereinafter also Josie or Jo) and thus both of my deceased siblings were commemorated in new lives. The coming of Nils interfered severely with Mother's role as breadwinner for the family. When I was older she told me that at one time during that fall her larder had been reduced to such an extent that she had only enough food remaining for breakfast the next day. She put the children to bed, prepared Father for the night, and then, alone, almost broke down. She wept, prayed, felt better, and retired, confident something would occur to help her go on.

About ten o'clock the next morning, Mr. and Mrs. Ditlev Holstad, who lived some seven miles away, drove up to the house and unloaded a large sack of flour. The Holstads, who lived near a settlement called Hader[8], owned a few acres of timber in the valley, and he had called upon us during the previous winter when he was on his land cutting trees. At the breakfast table that morning he told his wife of that visit with a family living in a dugout in the forest. He could not get us off his mind, became convinced we needed help, and determined to bring us provisions immediately. Mother always referred to that sack of flour as proof positive of the power of prayer and never again worried about food shortages or questioned divine protection of her and her family.

Rev. Muus, that indefatigable pastor, with many congregations in Goodhue and other counties in southeastern Minnesota, found time to visit the sick and infirm, and did so frequently. He cheered us up, administered communion, read the gospel, led us in hymns, and spoke the prayers. He was never in a hurry, everyone was important in his eyes, and his very presence seemed a benediction. He knew all our names, stroked our heads, and had a kind word for everyone. A selfless man, he was an outstanding pioneer pastor, and left a permanent impression on everyone he touched or encountered. He bestowed an atmosphere of sanctity and worship in any home he visited.

Nathan was confirmed in 1872 by Rev. Muus. My brother was then fifteen years old, eight years my senior. Shortly after his confirmation, the pastor visited our home to conduct communion services for my parents and, afterward, had a long conversation with them about Nathan's future. He told them the young man was talented and suggested they let him go to school to be educated for the ministry. That plan, if followed, would entail great sacrifice on their part for they would lose a potential breadwinner for the family. Worse, they had no funds to support Nathan while he would be in school. Impossible as the idea seemed, Rev. Muus asked my folks to not reject it out of hand but to give the suggestion prayerful thought. A few days later he returned and renewed his appeal. He kept a tutor at the parsonage for his own children and offered to take Nathan under his wing, place him with his children, and in that way prepare him for entrance to Luther College, located in Decorah, Iowa.

My parents consented to his plan but made it clear they could do nothing to help my brother financially. That condition was clearly understood by Rev. Muus. He nevertheless made room for Nathan, who spent two years in the parsonage (Holden Academy) preparing for college entry. In the fall of 1874, carrying all his belongings in a grain sack, my brother went off to Decorah and enrolled in Luther College. Rev. Muus kept in close touch with Nathan's progress, helped him find jobs during vacation periods, employed him around the parsonage when he could, and saw to it that he completed college and seminary studies. Nathan became a renowned pulpit preacher, an author, second president of St. Olaf College, (1899-1914) and lastly, Professor of Dogmatics at Lutheran seminaries in the Twin Cities. He was created a Knight of the Order of St. Olaf by King Haakon VII of Norway in 1905 and in 1912 the Augustana Synod made him a Doctor of Divinity. Nathan died September 25th, 1920, and is buried in Northfield.

7

MY UNFORGETTABLE
CHRISTMAS

The first Christmas tree I remember seeing was in
our dugout-log combination home. Nathan was home for
the holidays, had seen Christmas trees, and was determined
that we, too, should have one. There were no small, suitable
pines in our vicinity, but he eventually found one, cut it down,
and hauled it home on his shoulder. It could not have been a
very large tree, else he could not have managed to lug it, but
still, to me, after all the years that have come and gone, that
was the most wonderful Yule tree I have ever seen. A small
space was curtained off in a corner of our home and the tree
as well as Nathan disappeared behind the hanging. Secrets! I
heard noises, noticed the drapery move repeatedly, and was
very curious to know what was going on but no one would
tell me. Whatever was happening was meant to be a surprise.
Meanwhile, rice mush, lutefisk, flat bread, head cheese, and
syrup and bread studded with raisins, our Christmas Eve fare,
was being prepared. Despite the sounds and smells of cooking,
my mind was centered on that curtain: it seemed Nathan would
never finish whatever he was doing with that tree.

That afternoon it began to snow, perfect timing for
the night before Christmas. It came in large flakes slowly
and cautiously as if seeking places that needed to be covered
or were out of tune with the Yuletide spirit. The great trees

seemed like sentries on guard protecting the sanctity of the evening. All nature was hushed in honor of the occasion.

Every once in a while Mother would step outside for a long, searching look down the valley until, after one re-entry, she smiled in what to me was a mysterious manner. Soon my sister Matilda, down from Minneapolis, entered covered with snow and bearing a large package. She was greeted with smiles and joy, but the package, which, after welcoming my sister, had my full attention, went into the hands of Nathan, who ducked behind the curtain once again. My curiosity, fueled by his furtive behavior, nearly reached the bursting point. I remember Mother and Matilda carried on a long, intimate conversation in subdued tones and though I tried to over-hear what they were saying, their voices fell into ever softer levels, frustrating me even more.

Dusk was falling as was ever more snow, blanketing my great trees in glistening white. Mother began to look down the valley again and we all realized more surprises were in store for us. She began to fret, worrying about the food; it was getting late and the meal was about ready to serve. Finally, a man could be seen, faintly through the snow, slowly plodding his way up the valley towards the house. What suspense! Who could he be? He trudged nearer and nearer and suddenly I realized it was Andrew! Andrew, too, home for Christmas, stamping and shaking the snow from his clothes, greeted with laughter and joy by all. He had a sack over his shoulder, like Santa Claus, full of packages which disappeared as the others had behind that tantalizing curtain. Both Matilda and Andrew, we discovered, had walked the fourteen miles from Northfield, one behind the other only a short distance apart, neither knowing of the other's presence, and thus missed each other's help and companionship. Matilda had come by train from Minneapolis to Northfield, the nearest railroad station, and Andrew from his current carpentry job, I know not where.

When the joy of my sister's and brother's homecomings had subsided, Mother donned her silk kerchief and a white apron in honor of the convivial yet solemn occasion. The emigrant chest that served as a table was placed near Father's bed and dressed with Mother's finest napery and tableware. I always stood to eat, which was more comfortable than to sit, because the chest allowed no foot room at its base. We sang a Yuletide hymn, Mother read the Christmas gospel, followed it with the Lord's Prayer, and we ended our devotions with another carol before we ate our Christmas Eve supper. When we were finished at the table, the mysterious curtain vanished as if by magic and there stood a decorated and candle-lit tree, one of the most splendid sights of my childhood. The whole occasion was memorable because all my sisters and brothers, except Anna, were gathered together once again under one roof. Such a reunion would not happen frequently thereafter for one reason or another.

In the light furnished by the small candles on the tree, we gave all those packages our undivided attention. Gifts for everyone. I was given a many-colored scarf that went around my neck, crossed over my chest, and tied in the back. I insisted on wearing it all evening and wanted to take it with me to bed. I also got a pair of gray, homeknit mittens, a stick of candy, and half an apple. The tree candles did not last long and were carefully snuffed before the tree could catch fire, but the main lamp was replenished with a fresh supply of grease so we could stay up a little longer than usual. It was the happiest and most impressive Christmas of my life.

8

GREAT EVENTS OF 1872

I remember the year 1872 especially because of two events in addition to Nathan's confirmation and leaving home: the first involved the whole community and the second our family. The construction of Urland Church, erected on a site just a quarter of a mile from our home, in the midst of the forest (truly a church in the wildwood), was a boon to all in the neighborhood.[9] I went over there often to see the carpenters at work, wonderfully good men, I thought, because they were privileged to build a house of worship. My ambition, suddenly, was to be such a worker, each superhuman in my eyes, and I watched everything they did in order to learn how I, too, could build a church dedicated to God. Imagine my shock, then, when I overheard one of the men use profanity, cursing a bent nail. It seemed blasphemous that he could utter such words while engaged in his holy work, and I watched him carefully, expecting him to be struck down at any moment. But time passed and nothing happened to him, much to my surprise.

The second remarkable event of that year, affecting only our family, was brought about by an American, a "Yankee," as we called them, named Merritt, who lived farther down the valley. He took an interest in Father's condition and visited quite often, trying to learn Norwegian and teach us English, to enable us to converse more easily. When all of us could better understand each other, he brought another man with him whom he introduced to us as Dr. White. We soon understood he had brought the doctor to help Father recover his mobility. Communicating with signs and bits of broken English and Norwegian, we grasped that the doctor was interested in curing Father and would not charge a fee for his services. My father, persuaded, consented to an examination, and, as it proceeded, I watched keenly to see if Father made an attempt to leave his bed. After studying his patient, Dr. White applied an instrument I later learned was called "The Mechanical Resuscitator,"[10] to the fleshy parts of my father's body. The device resembled a shaving brush with needles in the place of bristles. When the instrument was placed against the flesh and a spring pressed in its handle, the needles pierced the skin. Following each puncturing, the doctor applied an oil to the area affected, resulting, the following day, in a patch of rash or small pimples where the needles had penetrated.

Dr. White returned ten days later and repeated the treatment, a service he performed thirty times in all, trying constantly to persuade Father to walk. After approximately twenty visits he brought Mr. Merritt with him and, together they lifted Father from his bed and placed him on his feet. Then, one man on each side of him, they carefully walked Father several times across the room and back. During the next visit, again by both men, the exercise was extended and Mr. Merritt was persuasive in encouraging Father to walk. I never knew why or how the treatment worked; moral suasion, the treatments themselves, or Father's fear of the device, but he walked, to the surprise of the community and the delight of his family. The walks, accompanied by me, were extended a bit each day the weather was favorable and as Father slowly gained confidence in his abilities. Word had spread through the neighborhood that the church builders would install a weather rooster atop the steeple on a certain day, and Father, wishing to witness the event, lengthened his strolls a little each day in preparation for the quarter mile hike to the new edifice.

When the great moment arrived, my father and I saw the rooster put in place and heard the church bell, installed some days earlier, toll for the first time—happy events for the community and especially for Father, for they seemed to herald his full recovery. Thereafter, with daily exercise and walks, his strength grew noticeably. In a comparatively short period of time he was able to rise in the morning and stay on his feet all day, with the exception of a short nap in the afternoon.

Dr. White's dramatic success with Father led to an extensive practice in the area, and my dad turned out to be the doctor's most valuable patient as word spread. My father was a walking, talking advertisement, living proof of Dr. White's competence and the efficacy of his wondrous machine. Many neighbors were cured of different ailments, mainly, I now believe, through the effect of the doctor's optimistic, encouraging, reassuring manner—a kind of power through positive, affirmative thought, an approach to healthy living popularized in the 1920s by Dr. Emile Coué and his "Every day in every way I grow better and better."[11] To this day I do not know if Dr. White was a qualified physician or a quack, but if he was the latter, his quackery was effective. However Father's recovery happened, we were grateful. It was not long before he was able to walk to the home of Mr. Meland, who made a great to-do over him and his miraculous recovery.

9

TWO GIFTED TEACHERS

Another man who stands out in my memory was our schoolteacher, Iver Davidson Hustvedt. I can see him still, that tall, lanky, kind, indefatigable man as he worked with us children of the community, teaching us to read and write Norwegian and to cipher. I think he was meant for the ministry and had missed his calling, for he was most interested in religious instruction. When he was engaged in that aspect of our education his earnestness and intensity transformed him into a different man, appealing and irresistible. He was also a trained and talented vocalist who taught us many hymns and tunes and some aspects of choral singing, as much as we could absorb. He used a tuning fork which all of us youngsters thought fascinating, some not quite grasping that the vibrations produced the sound.

Ours was a community school, not a public school in the modern sense, which would have prohibited the inculcation of a specific faith. In that earlier time, immigrants entered the nation without restriction or instruction in the American Constitution. It was only much later that our school changed to public status and Lutheran teachings were dropped from the curiculum, but when I attended it was a perfect forum for Iver Hustvedt, the would-be preacher who loved to teach.

We children, like most kids the world over, were not always models of deportment. We took advantage of his kind nature such as roaming in the woods surrounding the school during recesses, thus forcing him to round us up, or picking the clay from between the logs of the schoolhouse, a pleasant, though strictly forbidden, pastime; he seldom if ever lost his temper. Our faithful mentor, a patient, able, dedicated man, who worked for small thanks and less pay, devoted himself to his calling and to the children in his charge. Pastors of the church in the valley came and went but our teacher remained in the Urland community all his life.

Our schoolmaster, a member of Urland Church from its dedication to his death, quickly became Choral Director, leading the congregation in hymn singing, as well as the group's elected Secretary, which, over the ensuing years, evolved into Church Historian. No event of any importance escaped his pen, even in his old age after his hands were burned in a fire that destroyed his home. I remember him vividly, a bit shaky but still erect, towering over most men, at the congregational celebration marking his 84th birthday which I had the honor and pleasure of organizing.

That shepherd of the community, a gifted immigrant who contributed much in many ways to the development of his corner of America, passed away in November of 1931. On the 25th of that month people from the surrounding area gathered in and around Urland Church to escort their revered teacher and friend to his last resting place in the shadow of the house of worship he had loved and faithfully served all his life.

My oldest brother, Andrew, served his apprenticeship, was entrusted with ever more demanding work, developed into a skillful artisan, and had promise of becoming a master carpenter. Carpentry was much harder work in those days than it is now when boards can be ordered in any size or dimension. In the 1870s and 80s carpenters had to rip and shape boards from rough timber, using tools much inferior and slower compared to those we have today. He had to be skillful with the axe and adze, as well as with hammer, saw, chisel, and plane to do his work well. There were no specialists such as rough or finish carpenters (except cabinetmakers); one man did it all. In his apprenticeship Andrew was trained to build a complete structure by himself, if necessary, including making mortise-and-tenon joints[12] for locking beams together, window frames and casings, doors, stairways, railings, etc., as well as all trim. When he finished his training his services were in great demand and customers would delay building until he could do the job.

Andrew became almost a second father to me and taught me much that I know of the pragmatic aspects of life, including carpentry, of which my true father, preoccupied with his dubious health and his books, knew nothing. Circumstances and the dictates of his own nature made him a spectator all his life, incapable of practical pursuits. What I learned from my brother has served me well ever since, and the skills I acquired when I was young have given me a great deal of pleasure, for working with wood has been my principal avocation throughout my life. I gained, from my days with Andrew, a profound respect for hard work and learned a lasting lesson: never neglect an opportunity to gain a skill.

10

FAREWELL TO THE VALLEY

The growth of Luther College in Decorah, Iowa, founded and opened in 1862, was slowed by the Civil War. When the great conflict ended, the college soon flourished as a training school for young men who intended to enter the Lutheran ministry. Rev. Muus was keenly interested in nourishing the college and to do so began a preparatory school called Holden Academy[13] in his parsonage near Aspelund, Minnesota[14]. It was in this academy that Nathan spent two years, 1872-74, to ready himself for admission to Luther College. Holden Academy, in its short life, (1869-1874) had among its students many young men who later became leaders of the Norwegian Lutheran Church in America..[15] By the mid 1870s, Americans from Norway had thoroughly occupied northeastern Iowa, southeastern Minnesota, and were settling ever farther north and west in the latter state. Rev. Muus realized another college was needed in a location that would better serve the spreading immigrants. The capacity of Luther College would be reached in the near future and that fact, combined with the difficulties of travel at the time, indicated the need had come for another institution to be founded.

Pastor Muus and his associates, particularly Rev. Nils A. Quammen, minister to eight congregations near Farmington, chose Northfield, since 1866 the location of Carleton College, as the site of the new academy. They organized, incorporated, and named it for Norway's patron saint. The founding group of pastors raised funds for the new venture, acquired an abandoned public school building, cleaned and renovated it, and opened St. Olaf School on November 6th, 1874 for Holden Academy had nobly served its purpose and passed into history.

At the close of classes the following spring, Rev. Muus visited our home, told us about the new institution he and his friends had established in Northfield, and made a proposal. He suggested that our family should move there and open a boarding house for the students. Matilda and Andrew each had saved a bit of money that they invested in the enterprise. Rev. Muus, notified of the family's acceptance of his proposition, selected and rented a suitable house in town, (108 East Fifth Street) and provided wagons and teams for our removal to Northfield in the summer of 1875.

The day set for our departure from the valley came and with it a number of our nearest neighbors to say goodbye. Even though our home was only a dugout-log combination associated with disappointment, illness, poverty, struggle, and heartache, yet it was "home, sweet home," and it was not easy to bid it and our friends farewell. Mother, torn between eagerness for the new and nostalgia for the old, lingered so long about it that the teamsters became impatient and hurried her onto a wagon, and we were on our way to a different kind of life.

I was ten years old and that trip to Northfield was a delightful adventure. I had never seen a city, not even a town the size of our destination, or a railroad that I could recall. Filled with stories of trains and cities by my brothers and sisters, I was wide-eyed in anticipation. Nathan had told me there could be many sets of tracks side by side or there could be one pair, that the trains could be long or short, and that the locomotive might be placed in front or behind the cars, planting in my head all sorts of fantasies. Imagine my state of mind when I saw segments of a long freight train, seemingly unconnected, caused by flat cars hidden behind two small knolls between the train and the place we stopped to view it. Passing strange, I thought, but then, in regard to trains, I had been led to believe anything was possible, even magic. And the engine! So small but powerful enough to pull all those cars! Everything I saw and heard about that train made a lasting impression on me; it was the beginning of another life-long love, that of railroads, trains, and train travel—smoke, cinders, soot, and all.

11

NEW FAMILY IN TOWN

Upon our arrival in Northfield, we found Rev. Muus waiting for us to guide us to our rented house. After unloading our possessions and meager furnishings, he helped us procure the additional necessary furniture, and did everything possible to help us prepare to feed the students when the St. Olaf school term opened in the fall. One such good turn, a credit arrangement with a leading merchant made by Rev. Muus on our behalf, soured. My folks had some money, supplemented by the funds invested by Matilda and Andrew, both of whom had come to Northfield to help operate the boarding house, but it wasn't enough. Looking back, I realize now we were the perfect victims for any sharp operator, especially and unfortunately, by someone whom Rev. Muus admired, respected, and thought could do no wrong. Not only were we cheated, but the pastor's trusting nature was abused. The merchant, a pillar of society, and a member of the new school's Board of Trustees, arranged with my parents to let them have whatever they needed to start the business venture. In return they were to feed the merchant's clerks and hired men, thus paying him for the food supplies and merchandise he had advanced.

The plan seemed, at the outset, favorable and friendly. The storekeeper was solicitous for the family's welfare, promised a large discount, and even sent unordered items to the house until we were deeply in debt to him. His next step was to insist that we charge a low price per meal for his men or he would not send them to us and would demand payment in full. In that way he managed to get high prices for his goods. My parents soon wished Rev. Muus had not introduced them to their "benefactor," but in no way did they blame the pastor for their plight.

My folks struggled with that never diminishing debt. The merchant sent so many men to eat, they nearly crowded out the students who were our primary customers, and the price per meal was too small for any headway on debt retirement to be made. My parents wanted to raise the price per meal but dire threats ensued and demands were made for payment in full. Father kept our accounts but could never compare them with the merchant's records for one reason or another—he was always put off. The reduction of the debt was excruciatingly slow. I've often wondered why my father never informed Rev. Muus of the merchant's financial shenanigans, because I think he could have helped us. Perhaps Father felt we were already too obligated to the Pastor for his many kindnesses. The merchant's scheme was much like that used by company stores to keep workers hopelessly in debt and near poverty.

I was ten years old when I entered public school for the first time. All my prior education had been conducted in Norwegian by Mr. Hustvedt and I had very little English. I understood the teacher when she requested my name but I was at a loss when she asked me my age. A fellow student, Jim Murphy, tried to act as interpreter but he had about as much Norwegian as I had English. He did his best but it wasn't good enough, and to this day I believe my age was never entered into the school records.

When classes got under way, I mixed with the English-speaking students and it did not take long to learn the language. No other inconvenience or embarrassing situation arose in the meantime. My parents' difficulties with English contributed to their troubles with the boarding house.

During the winter tremendous snowball fights erupted between public school students and those enrolled in St. Olaf School. The battle lines were well drawn but there were charges and countercharges until it all came to a sudden halt. A snowball packed around a sizable stone hit a St. Olaf boy in the head and seriously injured him. From then on peace prevailed between the two groups of students.

Also that winter I acquired my first pair of skates. They were second or third hand and cost 25¢, a sum I earned by peddling handbills for two days to herald the opening of a new shoe store. The blades were fixed to wooden soles, painted red, and were kept on the feet by screws sunk in the heels of my shoes plus a strap over the toes. Eagerly I put them on, went out on an ice patch, but they were so dull I couldn't skate. Back to work I went, piled wood for a widow, and earned another quarter that went to a skate sharpener. With a good edge on the steel, the skates worked wonderfully well, but I never became proficient because my ankles were not strong enough to support the blades. My anticipation, though, had been so great I can taste it still. To obtain money to buy and then to have those skates sharpened I had worked for others and hadn't found it so bad. From then on I was on the lookout for odd jobs to earn spending money. I seldom if ever received any pocket change from my folks.

An eagerly sought source of income was associated with the late summer county fair held annually in Northfield. I got the job of carrying water from the river[16] to the animals on exhibition. It kept me busy but it was financially worthwhile. One day of the fair my little brother Nils was with me and we agreed to bring a barrel of water to a pastry booth in exchange for a pie. With the pie in our grubby fists we went to the river bank and, together, ate the whole thing. I don't remember about Nils but I soon had a severe stomach ache and through my pain learned another lesson: be moderate in all things. Pie was never quite as attractive thereafter.

12

THE FAMOUS NORTHFIELD BANK RAID

In slightly altered form, this chapter, titled "The Northfield Bank Raid," was published in Journal of the West, *Vol. XXIII, No. 3 (July, 1989) pp. 67-72. Reprinted with permission.*

The even temper of Northfield's daily life was violently shattered on September 7th, 1876, when eight men, dressed in linen dusters over riding clothes and mounted on splendid horses, rode into town. They stopped for lunch at a restaurant kept by Mr. Jackson, I was told, just below the Milwaukee passenger station,[18] where there is a lumber yard now [i.e., in the 1920s.] The men posed as cattle buyers and asked a lot of questions relative to that business. Their names, we and the world would soon discover, were Frank and Jesse James, Bob, Cole, and Jim Younger, Charley Pitts, Clel Miller, and Bill Chadwell. [Chadwell is also known as Bill Stiles, an alias (or vice versa.) The former name is used in my father's manuscript. Ed.] When they finished their meal, they rode up the street, across the city square, and over to the First National Bank. They had selected an opportune time to raid the bank because some of the best marksmen of the town were away on a hunting trip.

Jesse James, Cole Younger, and Charley Pitts dismounted and entered the bank. While one of the robbers stood guard over his and the trio's horses, the other four rode up and down the street, discharging their pistols into the air, and warning everyone to go inside.[19] It so happened that my father was in Harold Thoreson's store, only three doors from the bank. He stood just inside the front windows with others who were in the store and saw the bandits riding up and down the street as fast as their mounts could go. Suddenly, he told me, he saw one of the horsemen topple from his saddle directly across the street from Thoreson's. The man was Clel Miller, shot by Mr. A. R. Manning. Another robber, Bill Chadwell, fell in front of the bank, killed by Dr. H. M. Wheeler, later of Grand Forks, North Dakota. The physician shot through a second story window in the Dampier Hotel, which was located diagonally across the street from the bank, where the large brick block is now sited on the east side of the city square.

Our home and boarding house was the second house on East Fifth, a side street from Main where the bank was located. Mother was alone in the house. She was attracted to the front door by the shouting and shooting which she thought was an advertisement for a much ballyhooed children's show that was to take place that evening in Lockwood's Opera House, which stood opposite the First National Bank. When Mother was outside the door, a riderless horse with saddle and bridle came pounding around the corner from Main and passed the house. Soon another similarly equipped and following the first galloped by. A Dr. Goodhue, who had his office in the corner house, came out with a revolver in his hand and told Mother to go inside because the bank was being robbed. She told us later that she did not wait for another invitation to do so, and went down into the cellar but did not have the patience to stay there—too much excitement in the air.

When the bandits entered the bank, the teller, Mr. A. E. Bunker, whose wife was my schoolteacher, was about to go out the back door. He received a bullet in his right shoulder but escaped and entered the rear door of the hardware store owned by Mr. Manning whom he told what was going on in the bank. Mr. Manning selected a rifle from his stock of firearms, loaded it, and went over to the corner where he was sheltered by an outside stairway. He killed Clel Miller, whom Father saw fall from his horse. After the raiders fled, this stairway was found to be riddled with bullets.

Mr. J. L. Heywood was acting cashier, replacing the bank officer who was on vacation. When the gunmen ordered him to open the safe he told them that he could not do so. The robbers could see that the vault was provided with a time lock so they no doubt concluded that they had miscalculated the time it would be open. The story later on was to the effect that the vault was already unlocked, the door merely closed, and therefore Mr. Heywood could say truthfully that he could not unlock it.

By that time the gang members outside the bank were having a bad time of it. Two men and a horse were dead, two horses lost, and another bandit was severely wounded. The raider guarding the horses opened the bank door and told the men inside what was taking place in the street. The story is that the three men gathered up what loose change they could find and made for the door, giving up the raid as a bad job gone wrong. I was told that when Jesse James saw one of his men, Bill Chadwell, lying dead outside the door of the bank, he turned around and shot Mr. Heywood, who died shortly afterwards.[20] When they left town, one of the robbers [Bob Younger] was without a horse. He called to the others "For God's sake, don't leave me behind you." One of the men [his brother, Cole] then wheeled around and picked him up and so they departed, two brothers on one horse.

I was in school at the time. We heard the fire bell ring as well as some church bells. All of us children became very excited and clamored to go home. The teacher, Mrs. Bunker, went to see the principal about dismissing us. While she was gone, Mrs. Charley Drew came into the classroom to get her daughter, Belle, and she told us that the bank had been robbed and several men killed. When we heard that news, we did not linger for permission to go but ran as fast as we could to Main street, where we found two men and a horse lying dead. Mr. Heywood was dying in the bank and another man by the name of Anderson was dying in the hotel. He had tried to cross the street and, not understanding English, was shot for not heeding the bandits' orders to get under cover.[21]

The area near the bank was filled with excited people. Northfield, normally a sleepy little town, was wide awake. Everyone who had a shooting iron was suddenly brandishing it amid many brave declarations to the effect that if the speaker had only had a little more time not one of the raiders would have escaped. One of the St. Olaf students, a bully whom I disliked, was very fierce in his assertions of his own prowess. He swaggered about with an old, rusty gun in his hand and declared that if he had been present at the time of the holdup he would have killed them all. His room was in the school building, but about 11 o'clock that night he came to our home and asked if he could have a place to sleep as he did not like to sleep by himself at the school. He was admitted.

My sister Matilda was doing dressmaking for Mrs. Heywood that day, just at the time of the attempted robbery. They were out in the yard, getting a breath of fresh air, when they heard Mrs. Amery, across the street, telling her next door neighbor that the bank had been raided and that Mr. Heywood had been shot and might be dead. At this shocking and unexpected news, Mrs. Heywood fainted. Matilda and excited neighbors had a difficult time reviving her.

When the surviving six bandits escaped town, they rode in the direction of Dundas,[22] a village three miles south of Northfield. I heard later that the bags of silver coins they had managed to gather up in the bank proved too heavy to carry and were discarded along the road.[23] If that information is correct, the attempt to raid Northfield's bank was disastrous for the gang and had netted them nothing in return. Informed of events by telegram, some of the men of Dundas gathered in a saloon at the west end of the bridge [spanning the Cannon River] for the purpose of intercepting the robbers when they crossed, but the outlaws thundered over the bridge and up the street before the men in the saloon got their guns ready for action. I've always thought the townsmen were not too eager for the encounter anyway.

At that time there was a large and dense tract of timber, extending from Faribault to Mankato, called the Faribault Woods. Somehow, the six fugitives managed to disappear into that wilderness. They did stop to ask a doctor to examine their most severely wounded man. They told the physician to make short work of it because their friend had been wounded in a sharp encounter with the Northfield robbers, that they were hot on their trail, and had no time to lose.

The bandits spent about two weeks hiding in the woods while a huge posse searched the countryside for them. That fortnight it rained almost incessantly which added to the outlaws' miseries but also hampered their pursuers. At some point during that two week period, the James brothers deserted the other four, eluded all pursuit, and made their escape back to Missouri and its familiar haunts. The remaining four found their way to a forest-covered island in a large swamp a few miles from Madelia. Two of them went to a farm near the slough, owned by a man named Osborn,[24] to buy food. Whatever ruse they employed did not work because the farmer's son[25] realized they were two of the Northfield robbers. When the two men departed, he rode his horse as fast as he could to report his suspicions to the Madelia sheriff, who organized a posse, surrounded the island and, after some gunfire, captured the three Younger brothers. Another member of the gang, Charley Pitts, was shot and killed in the skirmish. The surviving Youngers were in miserable condition. They were taken to Faribault, Rice County seat, and locked up in jail. Ultimately they were tried, found guilty, and sentenced to life imprisonment in Stillwater penitentiary.

It speaks well for the citizens of Northfield that when there was some talk of breaking into the county jail and lynching the Youngers, a mass meeting was held and a resolution adopted condemning any action of that kind. Osborn's son, whose suspicions led to the capture of the outlaws, was handsomely rewarded. He was also offered a free education at the University of Minnesota, but, as far as I know, he did not enroll and seems to have dropped entirely out of sight.[26]

A couple of days after the attempted holdup the two bandits killed in Northfield were buried. They were placed end for end in one box and during the day of their burial were displayed in the city square for all to see. Towards evening they were interred in the extreme southeast corner of the old cemetery, before it was enlarged. I attended the funeral so I knew just where the double grave was located. The following Sunday I visited the site. I stood there for a while, thinking how hard it must have been to die as did these two men, when I noticed a lizard coming out of a hole in the grave. I was sure, then, that it was cruel to be a robber both in life and in death.

Since that time I have been told that Dr. Wheeler, who killed Bill Chadwell, opened the grave the night after the funeral and took the latter's body to the medical school he was attending for dissection. I have heard, too, that the doctor kept the skeleton of the man he killed in a closet adjacent to his office and that an uncle of Chadwell's, who lived near Grand Forks, Dakota Territory, came to the office to view his nephew's skeleton.[27]

Northfield was like an intoxicated man after the attempted holdup and it took a long time to sober up. The raid put Northfield on the map and it became a show place. People came from all over the country to view the bank, the bullet holes in the corner stairway from where Mr. Manning shot Miller, and the riddled window from which Dr. Wheeler killed Chadwell. More than thirty bullet marks and holes were found there. The failed bank robbery was, and still is, considered a significant event in the history of the town.[28]

I have detailed this narrative of the Northfield bank raid because I have read several accounts of it, but none of them is true. What I have related is what I saw and heard at the time of the attempted holdup.

13

MANITOU HEIGHTS AND FAMILY DEPTHS

St. Olaf School, located in an abandoned public building, was becoming popular, with both prospective students and townspeople. The latter wanted to encourage Rev. Muus and the other members of the founding group to keep the school in Northfield, and did so by subscribing between six and seven thousand dollars to be used to buy a permanent site for the institution. Manitou Heights, west of town, was then covered with timber and dense underbrush, part of a Mr. Cutler's farm holdings. He let it be known that the hill could be purchased and, after inspection and discussion, it was decided to buy the land and build a new St. Olaf School on the Heights. Thirty acres were acquired from Mr. Cutler for $1250.00 and that plot became the nucleus around which St. Olaf School [later elevated to college status] gradually increased its land holdings.

Rev. Muus was determined to raise $30,000.00, a minimum amount needed if the future college he envisioned was to get off to the right start. Other Lutheran pastors in that part of Minnesota did not have equal foresight and were not interested in the plan. Only the enthusiastic Rev. Nils A. Quammen of Farmington, who had helped establish the school in 1874, pitched in and gave Rev. Muus unstinting aid in raising funds for the new venture. Despite the apathy and disinterest of many colleagues, the two men calculated how much each farmer in the vicinity could give to the enterprise and persevered until they succeeded in obtaining that amount. By the end of 1876 they had raised $22,000.00, and a contract to build was let to Mr. C. P. Anderson for $18,500.00. Work was begun on June 4th, 1877, and when the cornerstone was laid and the building consecrated on Independence Day, the woods of Manitou Heights swarmed with people. The clerics in their robes, the consecration of the building, and the solemnity of the whole occasion made a deep and lasting impression on me.

On September 10th, the school authorities took possession of the new building, which later came to be known as "The Old Main," and the old schoolhouse, down town, was again abandoned. On November 6th, 1878, the fourth anniversary of the founding of St. Olaf School, the new building was dedicated by Rev. Muus. Four years earlier the school had opened with fifty students and now had almost doubled enrollment to ninety-nine, the year of its first graduating class.

The twice-abandoned school building in town was in bad shape. The city agreed to give it to the church school authorities, provided it was moved elsewhere. Coeducational from the beginning, St. Olaf had need for a Ladies' Hall. The gift from Northfield was accepted, the building torn down, and much of it used for the second structure on Manitou Heights. Andrew was employed in both the wrecking and rebuilding and, of course, I, then twelve years old, had to be present to be sure that things were done properly. The foreman in charge of the razing gave me the lightning rods from the old building. I sold the copper to a hardware dealer. It was a thrilling moment in my young life and represented the first of many benefits that would come to me from St. Olaf School and College.

One unpleasant consequence of the school's move to Manitou Heights was the closing of my parents' boarding house and the necessity of finding another means of livelihood. Unpleasant for the children but probably a blessing for my mother. After three years of practically round-the-clock work running the establishment, she was on the edge of collapse. She had tried to operate the business with as little hired help as possible and overtaxed her strength. When the boarding house was closed, the furniture, fixtures, and equipment were taken to Wang's store and sold at auction. Enough money was realized from that sale to pay all our debts, even what was owed to our grasping "pillar of society," and finance a move to a small house Andrew had built on the outskirts of Northfield.

We managed to keep going, during 1877-78, largely through the efforts of Mother, who procured a loom and did all the carpet weaving she could handle by working early to late, but her health, not fully restored after the boarding house closed, failed, and she had to take to her bed. Matilda contributed through her dressmaking skills and Andrew from his carpentry, but their incomes were not enough. Father, invalided as he was, could not do physical work, and contributed nothing to the family coffers. I had to quit school and go to work. I was 13 years old, in the fifth grade, and having to give up my schooling was a bitter disappointment to me. In my memory it remains one of the darkest days of my boyhood, but there was no alternative. I was fond of my teacher, a Miss Hathon, and couldn't bear to bid her goodbye. On the last day of classes, I watched my chance and slipped away when she was temporarily out of the room.

We were sunk in poverty and everyone knew it. Friends were not particularly kind or helpful; would-be employers were not always honest in their dealings with me; I discovered another valuable lesson—that outward appearances are important in building relationships with others. I have heard poverty extolled as a blessing in disguise. It isn't. That statement is nonsense. No one is better off because of poverty! Impoverishment is not a sin in God's eyes, nor a curse, but a blessing it surely is not, for the stigma of inferiority is its legacy that follows, hampers, and obstructs one's full development as a person all one's days.

My first employer never paid me for two weeks of hard work, a harsh introduction to the real world. I finally made some money when I worked in a cooper's shop[29] for 35¢ a day, in a planing mill for 70¢, and then, working from 7:00 A.M. until 6:00 P.M. in a flour mill, I earned the princely sum of $1.00 per day. The experience I gained there, however, was more valuable than my earnings. The owner of the mill was a Mr. John Ames, and at first he refused to hire me because of my age and size, and told me to go to school. But he was a kind man who had lost an arm in the mill and understood hardship. When he heard my story, he set me to work as a car loader's helper. The work, rolling and loading 220 pound barrels of flour into boxcars, was obviously too difficult for me. I persevered, though, and he, admiring my spunk, soon changed my work to helping the engineer with the heating boilers, which was much less physically demanding. Shortly, though, he shifted me to waiting on customers, making deliveries, and helping him as an interpreter. Mr. Ames treated his employees well, distributed barrels of apples and parcels of fresh meat to his men when those commodities were available or in season. Later on, unfortunately, he lost his mill because of alcoholism and left Northfield.

During 1878 we had visitors from Norway, fresh immigrants seeking land farther west. My mother's sister and her family, the Eldens, followed later by Peter Kaldal,[30] one of Father's brothers, and his family. The latter group went on to the area of Glenwood, Minnesota, and settled near my sister Anna Jermstad's home, while the Eldens journeyed farther north and found land about twenty miles north of Grand Forks, Dakota Territory, on the Minnesota side of the Red River of the North. The Red River Valley was the popular objective of many immigrants and we planned to go there too and take up a homestead. To prepare for the move, Andrew accompanied the Eldens in order to select and acquire land and build a log house before the rest of us followed him. Andrew did file on a quarter section (160 acres) of land near the Eldens, broke some soil, and found and hauled logs for a home, but all his efforts came to naught for the moment—Mother's illness temporarily prevented the family move.

During some of my scarce spare time I split and piled firewood for several well-to-do families, among them that of Mr. Norton, President of Northfield's Citizen's Bank. One day Mr. Norton questioned me about my family and our circumstances, which resulted, a few days later, in a visit to our home by him and his father, who was also in the banking business in St. Paul. The elder Mr. Norton wanted to adopt Josie and me. He and his wife, he revealed, were lonesome and were eager to share their large home in the capital city with two youngsters to whom they would give their legal name and would educate in the finest schools.

Another family council was held; our decision was a unanimous "nay." Jo, then almost eleven, and I did not want to leave our parents. Undaunted, the Nortons came again to our home, repeated the offer with added inducements, but we wouldn't budge from our decision. Josie and I wanted to remain Kildahls just as Nathan had done some years earlier when an offer was made to adopt him.[31] It seems we were attractive children to some townspeople, at least.

Mother, ill in bed, had consulted local doctors with little positive result. Through the good offices of Rev. T. N. Mohn,[32] she had been taken to LaCrosse, Wisconsin, to consult with a highly recommended medical man who was traveling from Oslo, Norway to settle in St. Paul. The great doctor could do nothing for her except recommend plenty of bed rest. Near desperation, for we could not bear the thought of losing Mother, Matilda remembered Dr. White, his treatment of Father, and the almost miraculous cure the good doctor and his marvelous machine had wrought. She learned that Dr. White was dead but got in touch with his widow who knew where to find the instrument and the oil her husband had used. A "Mechanical Resuscitator" and the necessary lubricant were procured and the ministrations were begun. Again, strange to say, the treatments proved beneficial; Mother began to improve, and soon was sitting up in bed, regaining her strength day after day to the family's delight. In a short period of time she was out of bed and walking, but, I'm sorry to say, she never became the strong and robust woman she had been prior to her illness.[33]

The family's hopes of moving north were revived. Mother was determined to acquire good land, build a home, and farm for our living. We thoroughly discussed the matter in family conclaves, with Mother adamantly insistent that she was strong enough to make the trip. A letter was sent to Andrew to tell him of Mother's improved condition and that we again planned to join him. In the meantime, Nathan, whose offer to quit school and help support the family had been turned down, was graduated (1879) from Luther College. That fall,

as he enrolled in Luther Seminary in Madison, Wisconsin, I
was included in the confirmation class under Rev. Mohn. We
planned to go north after I was confirmed the following spring
.

Rev. Mohn, pastor and educator, and Rev. Muus, a
pastor with visionary foresight, are the two best and greatest
men I have ever known. Both men helped my parents and
our family in every possible way, and the former not only did
everything in his power to aid my mother, but became a dear
friend to all of us. It is difficult to find words adequate enough
to thank those two leaders for all they did for my family. From
the time we came to Northfield, encouraged and assisted by
Rev. Muus, our lives were closely associated with St. Olaf
School, later College, and Rev. Mohn. When Rev. Muus
relinquished his support of us, the other pastor took hold and
continued the help we so desperately needed. They were both
magnificent men and outstanding shepherds of their flocks.
Rev. Mohn had a magnetic personality and was frank, open,
and generous to a fault.

A man of many parts, Rev. Mohn was instrumental in
founding a new church in Northfield while he was carrying
his administrative duties as President of St. Olaf School. I
remember very distinctly the meeting at which a small group
of men gathered with Rev. Mohn, in the old St. Olaf School
building, to organize a congregation. Father took me with
him because he disliked walking alone in the dark, as there
were few if any street lamps in Northfield in those days. At
the meeting, there was quite a prolonged discussion regarding
the name to be given the new church. It was finally decided,
on Father's motion, to call it St. Johannes (now St. Johns)
Lutheran Church. Rev. Mohn was called as the new church's
first pastor and Father was engaged as ministerial assistant, and
served in that capacity as long as we lived in Northfield.

14

CONFIRMATION AND TRAVEL PLANS

The year I attended confirmation class is memorable to me largely because I came to know Rev. Mohn. I had admired him from a distance, so to speak, but now came under his direct influence on a regular basis. I could think of nothing finer in life than to be like him. Eager that he should think well of me, I studied my lessons diligently to be always ready to answer any questions, because I did not want him to be disappointed in me. That year of confirmation preparation was both a rare opportunity to know this fine man and a revelation for me. Always an effective speaker, Rev. Mohn vividly pictured the responsibilities that we must face in future life, and pointed us toward high ambitions and aims. He inspired us to prepare not only for eternity, but for a full, rich, and useful life on earth. I think everyone in the class was thrilled by his words and imagery. We met in the new school building on the hill which gave us an opportunity to become acquainted with students, who told fascinating stories of school life and spurred my desire to be one of them someday.

Despite my $1.00 a day job, Matilda's dressmaking, Andrew's carpentry, and my other odd jobs, our family, as I indicated earlier, had difficulty making ends meet. Not all were as kind as Rev. Mohn who saw and addressed the person within the worn and ragged clothes that the individual may have been wearing. The lack of decent clothing plagued me most of my boyhood and youth. Too often the object of ridicule and scorn by other youngsters who frequently saw their discarded clothes on my back, I became defensive and self-conscious about my condition. My confirmation, on June 13th, 1880, was marred by the matter of attire. I had determined to have my own new

clothes for the event, but at the service my new duds appeared
cheap and shabby compared to all the others' clothes; my
mind dwelt on fashion rather than on the questions. I answered
adequately, however, and was confirmed, but because of my
shoddy appearance, truly so or merely imagined by me, I
avoided the group picture, an omission I regret to this day.

After I was confirmed there remained no reason why
we should not implement our plans to move north. Andrew, as
I mentioned earlier, had taken up a homestead near the Eldens
in Marshall County, Minnesota, on the Red River some twenty
miles north of Grand Forks. To secure the land he had plowed
some acreage and had staked out the claim, even though it
was on file at the land office. Andrew then had gone to Grand
Forks, found a small piece of land, and by June, 1880, in his
spare time, had nearly finished building a small house on the
site. He wrote that he would return to Northfield in the fall
to arrange our move to the Red River Valley. I remember the
family's anxiety caused by Andrew's letter, and the decision to
move that loomed. There seemed to be bad luck implicit in any
intended move by the family. Would another calamity, such as
Mother's illness, or a recurrence of Father's, occur to thwart
our plans? In retrospect, it seems we collectively held our
breaths, waiting for the other shoe to drop.

As the summer wore on, we became impatient. Almost,
it seemed, as if to hasten Andrew's coming, Mother went with
a friend back to Goodhue County and Urland Church to bid
old neighbors goodbye, and, of course, while she was gone,
Andrew arrived. I was sent with a team and wagon to find her
and bring her back posthaste to Northfield.

During that summer, Andrew had again found work
with Charley Anderson, the contractor who had bid on and built
the Old Main of St. Olaf School, or most of it. While the school
building was being constructed, Mr. Anderson, overextending
his resources, had built two fine residences in Northfield, and
had gone bankrupt. Unable to finish the Old Main, he went
to Grand Forks to find a fresh start but kept his family in
Northfield until he found a home for them in the north. When
Mr. Anderson departed Northfield, Andrew soon followed him,

for the former was a good boss who could find work for skilled hands.

Fall had come and Andrew and his employer planned to share a freight car to ship our respective sets of household goods. Grand Forks was in the midst of a lively building boom with Anderson and his right hand man Andrew in the thick of it, so they had little time to waste. It was getting late in the autumn and the northern building season would soon end, which added to their urgency. I found and brought Mother back to Northfield, our little house was quickly sold, and the boxcar was loaded with our goods. At next to the last minute Mother insisted on taking our cow and its calf with us, complicating matters and forcing Andrew to ride in the freight car as caretaker of our livestock.

We were all at the depot ready to go. The train was due to arrive around midnight when our old nemesis, the "pillar of society," the city of Northfield's leading merchant, and society's exemplar, appeared, arrogantly "ordered" the car not be coupled to the train, and demanded $25.00 which he claimed was owed him. Was this the dreaded second shoe everyone in the family expected to drop, preventing us from leaving? Our "benefactor" asserted he had not been paid in full because of a bookkeeping error. Andrew had worked out a settlement with the owner's accountant that, he thought, had satisfied all outstanding bills and debts. At the last moment, the merchant was not satisfied and demanded cash. We had just enough money to travel to Grand Forks but more funds had to be found somewhere if we were to depart on time. Andrew, overcoming his anger, consulted with Father, and together they went to Rev. Mohn's residence, found him still up despite the late hour, and negotiated a quick loan. They hurried back, paid the merchant in full, and finally we were free to proceed.

Andrew rode in the freight car with the cow and calf while the rest of us traveled in a coach, but all of us were happy to see the last of our nemesis, the pious proprietor, who had done his level best to keep our noses to the grindstone. All in all, our five years in Northfield were neither wholly good nor bad but merely a somewhat rough segment of life. I regret the impoverishment of our household, but some good times occurred too, and we had come to know some fine people as well as our share of villains. We had seen the Jesse James bank raid thwarted as well as St. Olaf School promoted, erected, and realized; I had worked for kind Mr. Ames and the gentle Nortons but we had run afoul of a sharp merchant; we had arrived with the help of Rev. Muus and departed with the aid of Rev. Mohn, two good and great men. I had been confirmed and was now, as we left to seek greener fields, on the edge of manhood. My memories of Northfield could not have been too bad because I was to return and remain for seven years to catch up on my schooling and attend both St. Olaf School and College, from where I was to be graduated in 1895, and where I was to find my future wife.

We arrived in St. Paul in the morning, sleepy, but happy to be on our way to a new phase of our lives. We stayed in the depot, waiting for an evening train that would take us to Grand Forks. Towards noon we saw Andrew sitting on the roof of our freight car as it was being shunted in the railroad yard. It was late in the fall with chilly weather upon us, and I remember Mother's concern for him. As mothers will, she worried he might catch cold or fall off the car, but nothing untoward happened to him. We left the capital city, population 33,000 according to the 1880 census, in the evening. Our trip north during the night and part of the next day occurred without noteworthy incident.

Andrew's small house, not quite completed, was located in the outskirts of the town. We found the house, moved in, and made ourselves as comfortable as we could while we waited for Andrew and the freight car to arrive. The next day, he and the train reached Grand Forks in the midst of a snowstorm. We were happy to see Andrew, the livestock, and our household goods, but not the storm, which created a serious problem; how to provide shelter for the cow and heifer until a stable could be rented or built. Luckily, a neighbor was kind enough to take them, temporarily, into his barn. The cow, which provided half our living, seemed like a member of the family, a member we all loved, and whose comfort and care were matters of great concern. When all our belongings, including the livestock, were secured in or near the house, we all shared a feeling of triumph. The land Andrew had selected was only twenty odd miles north and a winter away. When spring arrived, we would achieve our long hoped for objective—a farm of our own.

Yesterday's early season snowstorm was of short duration, the snow melted rapidly, and several weeks of lovely fall weather ensued. Grand Forks, as I indicated earlier, was experiencing a brisk building boom and Andrew arranged with his employer to hire me as a shingler. My brother earned $3.00 per day and Mr. Anderson paid me $2.00, a 100% raise over my best wage in Northfield, and I felt wealthy. This income, together with Matilda's earnings as a dressmaker, enabled us to purchase some hens and a rooster. Eggs were very expensive at that time and our chickens, cared for by Father, more than paid for themselves. That winter the family managed to get along quite well.

During our leisure time during the cold months, we gave thought to our coming move to the farm. We planned to buy a pair of oxen, then Andrew and I would go down river to the farmstead, finish the house Andrew had barely begun, and then move our parents, the children, and the livestock to the farm. Andrew and Matilda would then return to Grand Forks to earn enough to keep us all alive until we could realize some income from the farm. This was a good plan but there was a hitch—I knew nothing about farming. But I was willing to learn, and did, and later we followed this plan fairly closely.

In the meantime, my brief experience in a cooperage shop in Northfield came in very handy both in shingling and, when cold weather drove me inside, lathing.[34] I continued with this work in unheated houses until winter truly set in shortly before Christmas, bringing intense cold and heavy snowfalls. All carpentry work was suspended until spring and while we waited for the end of winter, Andrew and I worked at whatever odd jobs we could find.

In the fall of 1879, the year before we arrived, Grand Forks had a population large enough to boast of fourteen children of school age, and a makeshift school, with one teacher, was opened. The inadequacy of this arrangement was soon evident as settlers, like us, began to arrive in large numbers. In the fall of 1880 a proper schoolhouse was built and one of the winter jobs I obtained was to operate the heating plant of the new structure. It was necessary to keep the building warm enough to finish plastering. The little experience of operating boilers that I had gained in Mr. Ames's flour mill in Northfield enabled me to land that job. Everything I had tried or learned earlier was turned to good advantage in our new home.

The population of the new city was about 75% Norwegian, with more arriving daily, and most business was conducted in that language. There was a popular story that made the rounds, probably repeated in other settlements, that the first post office had only four pigeonholes; one each for the Olsons, the Johnsons, the Knutsons, and the Miscellaneous.

The residents of Grand Forks were unusually sociable. From Christmas to New Year's Day was one continuous holiday, celebrated by a great deal of sharing by those who had plenty with others less well-off. Many families held open house to which all were welcome. There was a conscious effort by the wealthier people to be sure everyone had the means to celebrate New Year's Day and start the New Year right, a warm and gracious custom now neglected.

Grand Forks was an important station for the heavy river, ox cart, stage, and even dog team traffic between the Twin Cities and the Red River Valley settlements. That traffic died out when the railroads came, but we saw some remnants of the different modes of transportation. It is hard to believe now, but in those days there was a regular steamboat traffic on the Red River, one of only two or three major rivers in the United States that flow north. The boats went from Fargo down river to, then through, the length of Lake Winnipeg onto the Nelson River which flows northeasterly to its outlet in Hudson Bay near York Factory, Manitoba. When Captain Grigs docked his S. S. International, Captain McCormack his S. S. Selkirk, or Captain Viet his S. S. Minnidak at river towns they usually created a great deal of excitement. The Captain of the most majestic ocean liner never looked prouder than these men did when they approached landings with flags flying, deep-toned whistles sounding, and bells ringing. I was a lad and, of course, I was impressed, not so much by the steamboats, which were quite small, but by their captains. They wore startling, pretentious uniforms which certainly gave them an air of authority, and when they bellowed orders in resonant voices everyone within hearing knew, without doubt, that they were steamboat captains.

Flamboyance and comic pomposity aside, those captains were honest, rugged, forceful men, important contributors to the development of the nation. The coming of the railroads doomed the little steamboats but in their heyday they created a colorful era in our history. The three captains, no fools, saw and read the handwriting on the transportation wall, and hedged their futures. Captain Viet owned and operated a flour mill and Captain Grigs bought a sawmill which met much of the insatiable demand for lumber by the city's burgeoning population. Ultimately, the three men became proprietors of hotels in Grand Forks.

The industries that were dominant in Grand Forks when we arrived, were Mr. Viet's flour mill, Mr. Grigs's sawmill, (both of which occupied more and more of each man's time as steamboating died) building and construction, and land speculation. While weather permitted, my brother and I worked as carpenters, but, as I mentioned above, we were forced to quit that activity shortly before Christmas, 1880. After the holidays, I approached Mr. Viet and applied for a job. Now my flour mill work experience in Northfield became valuable because, on the strength of it, he hired me. I welcomed the opportunity, but unfortunately for the captain, (as well as for me) another, larger mill was built that put him out of business. The new enterprise produced "Cream of Wheat," a breakfast cereal that became immensely popular throughout the nation and world, and still is.

Grand Forks in 1880 was a pioneer town where the acquisition of, or speculation in, land was a contagious preoccupation with everyone and the subject of endless conversations and conjectures. It was difficult in those circumstances to keep my ambitions and goals in perspective. I wanted land but only for the purposes of enabling my parents to live from it as well as to provide a financial source for my education. It would have been easy to succumb to the prevalent land madness and settle for being a land-rich farmer for the rest of my days, but that really wasn't what I wanted to do with my life. Rev. Muus and Rev. Mohn had reached deeply within me, stirring feelings and kindling ambitions, and I was determined to satisfy my hopes and desires, if at all possible.

As if he was meant to reinvigorate my plans to prepare for the ministry. in late winter a third influential man touched my life. We were visited by Rev. Ole H. Aaberg, a pioneer Norwegian preacher in Dakota Territory,[35] to invite us to a meeting he planned to hold in the auditorium of the courthouse the following Sunday evening. I became interested in him, not because he was like Rev. Muus or Rev. Mohn, but because of his determination to minister to settlers in the west. I remember

I went to the courthouse the next Sunday and helped him build a fire that we kept going until the time came for the service he was to conduct. It was a small audience that came that evening but it was the beginning of a congregation that grew, organized, and later built a church. That procedure of founding and building congregations became Rev. Aaberg's primary work. He was not dynamic or authoritative; neither eloquent nor forceful. He was, at best, a mediocre pulpit preacher and was, perhaps, too humble. But he had vision and a missionary zeal that gave me a new insight on life and a new slant on the ministry. My desire to become a pastor was intensified. I could not dare even to think of aspiring to the level of a Muus or a Mohn, but a ministry such as Rev. Aaberg's seemed attainable. My ambition to go on to school also became more compelling with his encouragement. He became a dear friend of our family and kept in touch with us for many years. He will make another appearance later in this narrative.

15

FARMING, FRIENDS, AND FIRE

The winter of 1881 is memorable to many, especially to those who lived in or near Grand Forks, for the tremendous amount of snow brought to us by seemingly endless snowstorms. The vast amount of snow resulted in an unusually wet spring. The Red River's flow to the north was blocked by ice and, with no outlet, the river spread for miles, flooding the countryside and the people in it. In those conditions, getting to our farmland was going to be a problem, I thought, but Andrew had ideas on the subject and they worked out precisely. We bought lumber for the house to be built and, using the boards together with some logs, he and I made a raft which we floated down the river twenty odd miles to the very spot where Andrew planned to build the house, the only dry area on the acreage. The farm was located near the present site of Oslo, Minnesota, on a peninsula formed by the Red River on the west and the Snake River, a tributary of the Red, on the east and north. The combined flood waters of the two streams created what seemed like an inland sea.

By the time the flood subsided, we had the house built. My brother and I returned to Grand Forks, packed up the family, household goods, and livestock and moved up to the farm. To behold the joy our mother derived from the move was worth all the work it entailed. She had longed for a farm for years and could hardly believe that her dream had been realized. In accordance with our plan made during the winter, Andrew and Matilda returned to Grand Forks to continue with their jobs while the rest of us would farm. Andrew had, as I mentioned earlier, plowed a few acres on which we meant to sow wheat, but too many growing days had been lost while the land was under water, and that forced us to plant oats. This was a disappointment; wheat commanded much the better price of the two, but, almost as compensation, we harvested a bountiful crop of oats. I'm still proud of my first crop because I knew little or nothing about farming. Our neighbors were most helpful, willing to teach me what they knew, and it wasn't long before I felt more at home on the soil. Mother soon decided that our land was better suited for stock and dairy farming than for raising grain. The countryside was covered with a magnificent crop of wild grass, a ready-made supply of hay for our livestock, which had grown in number. She proved to be correct in her appraisal of the farm.

One neighbor in particular, Per Skavlem, knew a great deal about farming and helped me no end, by advice and example, to learn my new occupation. The Kildahls did not have the funds to hire help, nor did Per, so we joined forces, and with two teams of oxen and his hay wagon we cut and gathered a great abundance of hay for both our farms. Per, an ignorant man, huge as a bear, but kind and bighearted as daylight, would do anything for us. Happy to have close neighbors, he showed it by helping me haul logs from the timber stand, by sawing wood, building a stable, and digging a well. A strong, capable, practical man, Per taught me many valuable lessons about farming and stock raising. We nominally worked together but in fact he did most of the labor.

My first attempt to drive oxen was an unforgettable experience; I didn't drive them, they drove me. In hot weather they, precipitously, would leave the furrow I was plowing, and, dragging plow and me in their wake, make for the nearest water, a little pond some distance away. Without ado they would wade into the middle, stand still and, I came to think, look mischievously at me while I did all I could to coax them from their refreshing hoof and leg bath. Once—oh, maybe twice, I gave up the struggle and joined them.

The flood was not an unmixed disaster—it did us the service of exposing ridges and depressions in the terrain. We discovered that most of an uninhabited section just north of us was above water while a large portion of our land was submerged. We determined to secure that high and dry area as soon as possible. We drew up grandiose plans to use that section for grain and keep our present acreage as a dairy farm.

Alas, all our dream castles collapsed: the section we coveted was reserved for a school and was not available.

In the fall when the grass was dead and dry, we could see prairie fires in every direction. Per helped me plow two concentric rings of eight to ten furrows each around our buildings with the intention of burning off the grass between them. I found that achieving that goal could be a tricky business for while I was about it a strong wind suddenly arose and carried the fire over the outer furrows onto the prairie. Fortunately, the fire jump occurred on the north side of our buildings and the south wind rapidly spread the flames in a northerly direction for eight or nine miles. Without warning the wind shifted from the south to the northwest and the fire, instead of dying on its own ashes, swept southeast for about ten miles. Unless one has experienced such a sight, one has no idea of the sense of helplessness, and terror, it inspires. I was relieved to see the flames finally die, but I was afraid someone would be mightily interested in discovering who had started the fire. After a few days, I realized that apparently no harm had been done and I relaxed. Fires were common and widespread during the autumn, as I mentioned earlier, and evidently no one was particularly surprised or upset because of one more.

My unexpected fire jump luckily did no harm to anyone, but my cousin, Adolph Elden, through delay, lost his entire hay supply to the flames. He was absent from his farm doing some other kind of work, but had arranged with a neighbor to plow firebreaks around his hay stacks. Unfortunately, the friend either forgot or was delayed in doing the favor, and fire, waiting for no man, made the work unnecessary. All the neighbors got together and arranged a hay hauling bee in which Per and I took part. About noon on the designated day each neighbor, for many miles around, arrived at Adolph's place with a load of hay, thus insuring the survival of his livestock through the coming winter.

A haying bee offered the opportunity for a rare get-together and an occasion for a party that began with a sumptuous meal followed by a seemingly endless supply of liquor called "alcohol punch." Its ingredients evidently were a great deal of alcohol and very little punch, whatever that was. The concoction was too strong for many, who wisely chose to burn away the strong fumes before consuming it. Others, short of matches or patience, drank it as it was, contributing to the orgy that ensued. It reminded me of stories of the drinking bouts held by the Vikings of old. People collapsed and soon the rooms were crowded, impromptu dormitories with dead-drunk men sprawled in every direction, "sleeping it off."[36]

One of the men did his utmost to get me to drink by coaxing, threatening, and ridiculing me until another participant, a bit more sober, prevailed upon him to leave me alone. From what I saw that afternoon and evening I concluded alcohol consumption could not possibly be good for people's health, wellbeing, or happiness. No one I saw who was drunk looked very happy—they looked miserable. I vowed then and there never to touch the stuff as long as I lived. Some of the drinkers were in such bad shape, I thought surely they would die. But the human frame can absorb even that severe punishment and recover, much to my sixteen year old surprise, to live and drink another day.

16

THE RED RIVER: FLOODS AND BRIDGES

During winters strong winds caused snow to drift in our yard and nearly buried the stable and haystacks, making cattle chores a true hardship. Blizzards, accumulating immense force across the open plains, were so fierce we had to stretch a wire from the house to the stable to enable us to find our way from one to the other. Without such a wire or rope to guide us, we could easily become disoriented and wander blindly, all sense of direction lost, and finally, exhausted, die of exposure. Every winter there were instances of just such occurrences. We soon learned it paid to be prudent when blizzards descended upon us.

Heavy snows that winter caused a repetition of flood conditions in the spring of 1882 that we had suffered the year before, again necessitating late seeding. The same natural disaster recurred in the spring of 1883, but that inundation was, marginally, the worst of the three we lived through. Conditions were so bad we had to erect a platform of logs for the cattle to keep them from drowning. Our only means of movement around the farmstead was by boat and as we floundered about, fish from the Red or the Snake Rivers were blithely swimming over the golden grain fields of our dreams.

Three years of that kind of non-farming exhausted the patience even of my long-suffering mother. We had been yearning for land, and good land we had but in an impossible location. We had no choice but to plan another move to a dryer place and give up some of the richest soil in the world with a timber stand close by as a source of fuel and lumber. If some way is ever found to control the annual flooding, that land will produce varied and abundant crops. I've often thought how easily we could have moved in another direction when we left Northfield. Eastern Iowa, for example, offered a slightly milder climate, a longer growing season, closer markets, and more valuable land. Every aspect of our lives would have been less taxing and more satisfactory, and yet, as with many other settlers, we seemed to be driven or drawn in a northwesterly direction, almost as if we had no control over our movements and were caught in a kind of communal urge to go that way.

People seeking land were going farther west to find it and in 1883 the Devils Lake area in Dakota Territory was just opening up to settlement. No one knew much about it but the subject was a popular topic of conversation. Faced with an impossible situation on the banks of the Red River, we, too, succumbed to the land fever, and that spring Andrew, always the family's lead scout, went west to explore Devils Lake and the land around it. He was favorably impressed with what he found and promptly staked out three quarter sections on land neither surveyed nor yet placed on the market by the federal government. In those circumstances, the only way to claim and hold the land was to "squat" on it; i.e., live on it, mark the corners with stakes or stones, and plow a furrow around its borders.

Andrew returned highly elated with the new prospects and the family infected with his enthusiasm, decided that he, Matilda, and I should drive out there with the oxen and establish a new home. Mother had misgivings about the arrangement but, although not feeling well, faced the hopelessness of our present circumstances and finally acknowledged that we had no choice. Worried that she might die before our return to move the family, she insisted we make preparations with that contingency in mind. We divided our few pieces of furniture and other household goods and took half with us as well as the plow, the hay rake, and most of the cattle. With some urgency, spurred by Mother's forebodings, we bade goodbye to her, Father, and the children, Josie and

Nils. We began our trek to the Devils Lake area on June 3rd, 1883.

All signs were propitious—the weather was fine, the road along the river was in good condition, and we reached what is now East Grand Forks, Minnesota in short order. There was no need to ford the river to get to Grand Forks because there was a bridge of sorts we planned to use. When steamboats vanished from the Red, by 1882 or thereabouts, and for a few years thereafter, the bridge we intended to use consisted of a river barge placed crosswise, held fast by cables. It made contact with land at each end by means of broad gangways connected to the barge by hinges, which meant the angle of incline of the gangways varied with the rise and fall of the river. That "bridge" served very well in normal conditions, but when the river was low or in spate there should have been a "no bridge" sign on each bank to save travelers a lot of trouble.

A great deal of traffic was moved by oxen. Those economical, dependable, and powerful friends of the pioneers contributed a great deal to the establishment of farms and the growth of fortunes in the Red River Valley. They, and the wagons or carts they pulled, are the original "Empire Builders."[37] But, they had limitations, too, and one of them was the inability, when the river was high, to climb the steep incline of the gangways to the barge-bridge, or, when the water was low, to negotiate the decline. I have seen one driver after another try to make the crossing under such conditions only to give up and remain where they were in bad temper and after exhausting their sometimes amazing vocabularies of impolite language.

Occasionally, when the river was low, a driver would manage to get his team and wagon down onto the barge-bridge but was unable to leave it because the incline at the other end was too steep. He had escaped, say, Minnesota, but was barred from Dakota Territory, caught betwixt and between. It was only a matter of time until some enterprising fellow, his name lost to history, helped travelers and their teams up and down the gangways, kept the traffic flowing, cleared the air of all that blue language, and generally benefitted everyone concerned, not least, of course, himself. He made a tidy income from his activities, a true American entrepreneur who saw his opportunity and seized it.

The old barge-bridge was in existence for a relatively brief period. As population grew the river level steadily dropped and the barge finally came to rest on the river bed. It remained a monument to the river's earlier size but was replaced with an honest-to-goodness bridge as we have come to know them. Gone are the days when a barge of its size could easily be floated in the Red but twice I have seen the river five miles wide. Bringing in the barge to serve as a bridge during a flood presented no problem. When the three steamboat captains became hoteliers, they may have had something to do with creating a barge-bridge to hasten and increase traffic from the east. When we arrived at the bridge, we encountered no problems; the river was at the perfect level to keep the gangways flat with the bridge at both ends, or nearly so, and we crossed into Dakota Territory in the late afternoon, but still in time to purchase some provisions. We planned to start west early the following morning from the house Andrew had built on the outskirts of Grand Forks in 1880.

III

DAKOTA TERRITORY

John N. Kildahl, Nilsine J. Kildahl, and Harold B. Kildahl, Chicago, 1909.

The Kildahl family, circa 1885..

17

STOP, START, AND TRAILS WEST

Our plan for an early start on June 4th had to be changed. During the night it rained heavily, making the roads impassable and forcing a layover. We were lucky to have the small house still available, although Andrew had had offers for it and, tentatively, had accepted one, but, as yet no cash had changed hands. Real estate of any kind was in great demand, and he anticipated no trouble in making a fast sale, which he did the morning we left for the west. However, during that day of enforced idleness we saw some strange sights caused by the incomparable Red River mud, a goo in a class by itself. Among the phenomena we saw was a team of strong horses hitched to a light, single seated buggy, hopelessly stalled in the main street; another buggy with wheels apparently made of mud; merchants transporting goods from the train depot to their stores in hand wagons on the sidewalks, avoiding the hopeless bogs called streets. One hardware dealer, moving kegs of nails in that way, had the misfortune to lose a keg into the morass and watch it disappear from sight. It took much time and great effort to bring it to the surface and retrieve it. Not that day but on another occasion I saw a pig so immersed in mud on de Merse Avenue that only his snout appeared above the surface, but it didn't seem to mind—it was grunting most contentedly, truly in a pig's paradise.

The next morning, not waiting for the ground to dry out, Andrew found his buyer, gave up the house key, signed a paper in exchange for cash, and we left Grand Forks. We made quite a procession as we plodded west toward Devils Lake. The oxen, ill matched, with the lean, lank, nervous one always a couple of feet ahead of his fleshy, stoic, and slow partner, pulled the wagon loaded with our goods, plow, and the three of us. Tied behind the wagon was the hay rake and tied to that was the cow, followed by the young stock walking in single file. We followed a dirt road that grew fainter as the distances between human habitations steadily increased and the prairie became less and less marred by the hand of man. Our vehicle was not a covered wagon called a "prairie schooner," but a boxy, all-purpose affair which served our needs and uses very well. We had a large piece of canvas with which we covered ourselves at night, and, if it rained, we tied the livestock to the wagon and made our beds on the ground under its floor.

One evening, all of us tired out, we happened to stop the wagon over a slightly inclined depression, the wheels astride an old buffalo trail. If any of us had been alert we would have paid more attention to the terrain, but, eager to make a fire, eat, and bed down, we missed the signs of potential trouble. Before turning in we suddenly became aware that the skies were clouding over and we thought it prudent to tether the livestock to the wagon and sleep on the ground under its floor. During the night a sudden heavy rain turned our slight depression into a small lake. We were thoroughly soaked but could do nothing about it until the rain ceased. Fortunately, we had kept our day clothes dry by putting them in nooks and crannies we found on the underside of the wagon bed above our heads and changed to them as quickly as we could after the weather cleared.

Comfortable again, we watched the sun rise in all its June glory. The sky cleared, a great number of meadowlarks greeted the new day, and the air was laden with the sweet smells the prairie exudes following a soaking rain. Suddenly it was a glorious world, redolent of friendship and good will, bidding us welcome to the West and all its possibilities. Forgotten was the unpleasantness of the night as we enjoyed the moment. We took more time than usual to prepare and eat breakfast after spreading out and draping, where we could, our wet bedding. There was no rush to hitch up and roll that morning, enthralled as the three of us were with the sheer joy of living. Anyway, our bedding was slow in drying. The farther west we traveled the more abundant became our food supply in the form of small game, especially ducks, snipe, and rabbits. We saw the heads of antelope occasionally but they were extremely cautious and too swift of foot for Andrew to get near enough with his rifle to bring one down. Although I would have appreciated a taste of antelope meat, I must confess I was secretly glad he couldn't get close enough to kill any of those magnificent creatures.

Others, of course, were traveling west too and once in a while our strong, plodding oxen were obliged to pull somebody's horse-drawn wagon out of a muddy place. Numerous times such outfits passed us, often with supercilious or derogatory remarks about our slow animals cast quite gratuitously in our direction. Horses, however swift, can become helpless in deep mire, and so it was with some joy and assertions of superiority (un-Christian, true, but supremely satisfying) when we would catch up with one of our tormentors, hopelessly bogged down, waiting for us and our oxen to pull him and his rig out of the muck. The efficiency and strength of our animals put an end to the smart remarks. If it was an especially heavy load that was sunk in mire, we would substitute harnesses for the yoke and the oxen never failed in their duty, eliciting warm smiles, heartfelt thanks, and even some kind words for our ungainly beasts.

Three years had passed since I first worked with oxen. I had learned some lessons about those faithful beasts. We did not lead them. As a rule they obeyed orders. "Ha" meant turn to the left; "Gee" told them to turn right. Sometimes we would walk beside them on the left side of the team. After a young steer was broken in, he generally kept to the road. If they were properly broken in they would even turn out of the road when they met oncoming traffic but on occasion they needed persuasion from the touch of a long whip. When plowing, the "off" ox, or the one on the right side, walked in the furrow and stubbornly remained in it except when he smelled water on a hot day, a circumstance I have described. The ox on the left side was called the "near" or "nigh" ox. Oxen were quite intelligent, and always obeyed the word "whoa" which meant "stop." If they did not obey the "ha" or "gee" we would jump off the wagon and apply the whip. Very heavy hauling required a yoke, otherwise a harness was used which gave the animals somewhat more freedom in movement. It never paid to raise one's voice with oxen, which would merely excite them and might make them balk. It was best to talk gently and kindly to them and pet them when you wanted their best efforts. Almost always, then, they would give you every bit of strength they possessed.

18

BARTLETT, DEVILS LAKE, AND MR. CHURCH'S FERRY

Bartlett was the railhead (temporary terminal) of the Great Northern Railroad at that time. About half way between Grand Forks and Devils Lake, it was the most wide open town I have ever seen. Later, in 1889, when Dakota Territory was divided, North Dakota was admitted to the Union as a dry state, but no prohibition was evident in Bartlett in 1883. It seemed the town was composed exclusively of saloons, gambling houses, and brothels. As luck would have it, I encountered a young man I had known in Grand Forks, and had wondered what had become of him. After greeting each other, he took me to his place of business and introduced me to his partner, a madam it turned out, and together they were operating one of the busiest saloon-brothel-gambling house combinations in Bartlett. I had always thought of him as a fine young man but it seems I hadn't really known him at all. He had a weakness for gambling and, unfortunately, had won a large stake in a game in Grand Forks, enough for him to invest in his present business.

Obviously, he was proud of his accomplishment, but I could feel nothing but disappointment in him as I watched the Indians, cowboys, and soldiers, who packed the place, get drunk, lose money gambling, and end up in the not so tender care of the madam and her girls in the third part of the establishment. My erstwhile friend and the woman were coining money around the clock, but it was an evil, highly offensive business, and one all too common on the frontier. There were a great number of drunks and would-be desperadoes in the town and we thought it best not to stay there, so drove on a few miles west and camped rough for the night.

Bartlett never grew. The Great Northern Railroad authorities intended to make the town its temporary terminal and, as I indicated earlier, while we were there it was the railhead. However, the townsite company was too unreasonable in the price of its land, an extortionate scheme the Great Northern authorities rejected. They broke off negotiations, bought land a few miles west of the town, and extended the roadbed to the new site. Houses under construction were abandoned and others, one by one, were moved to the new townsite until all hope for the great future of Bartlett died. Later that summer the Great Northern extended its tracks to Devils Lake City.

We continued our journey from our camp west of Bartlett and, traveling an average of twenty miles a day, it took us five days from Grand Forks to reach Devils Lake City, a pretentious name for a community consisting of a few shanties. It was the westernmost semblance of a town in northern Dakota Territory; towns came into existence only as a railroad's thrust westward opened land to settlement. Although the Sioux were pretty well subdued, we heard rumors that occasional bands of Crow Indians could still make life miserable for the unwary newcomers who got too far ahead of the Great Northern railhead.

Farther south, the Northern Pacific Railroad was all but completed and the Indians and the countryside were considerably tamer. Devils Lake City had been sited in expectation of the railroad's arrival but the same error was made as had occurred at Bartlett: too much money was wanted for land. The Great Northern simply shifted its roadbed to the northwest and established a terminal on cheaper land. Just as Bartlett had withered away, so did the old Devils Lake City as its buildings were moved to catch up with the railroad.

Devils Lake City had to move itself only about a mile. By fall of 1883 it was a proper town and growing in the typical western manner, which meant it soon had a full complement of saloons, gambling halls, and brothels. But houses were built, too, and Andrew, employing his carpentry skills, worked on one after another until the cold weather forced him to quit. His income meant much to us as we had only his proceeds from the sale of the Grand Forks house, plus a bit Matilda had accumulated with which to start farming. The money he earned would go a long way in setting us up in business.

In 1883, the main body of water constituting Devils Lake was forty to fifty miles long by about twelve or so miles wide. It was a small inland sea with old Fort Totten[38] and the Indian reservation on the south shore and the beginnings of Minnewaukon at the west end. Devils Lake City did not border the lake so the railroad laid a spur track from the town to the head of Creel Bay. A boat landing was built and soon the steamship Minnie H plied between the fort and the two growing towns.

There was considerable lake traffic for several years, but, as the land became cultivated, less and less water flowed into the lake, diminishing its size, and finally eliminating boat traffic. Another factor contributing to the demise of steamboat travel on the lake was the extension of the Northern Pacific Railroad system north from Jamestown to Leeds with a station at Minnewaukon. When we first arrived, there was a large lake but no towns and now there are small cities but no lake, which disappeared over the years.[39]

Life was hard and justice prompt in Devils Lake, (the word City was soon dropped,) as it was in much of the west at that time. In one instance I remember, two brothers named Ward jumped a claim near the town. When the original claim holder came home to his land in the spring, he found a new shanty on the far end of his property. His response to this challenge was swift, simple, and deadly. He went back to Devils Lake, set up drinks for a crowd, who, worked up a little, went out to the claim and shot the Wards to death. With so many men shooting it was impossible to prove whose bullets actually killed the brothers and the case was dropped. Another man was killed for jumping a claim, but whether a bullet or heart failure caused his death could not be determined, and the killer, defended by a celebrated St. Paul attorney, was acquitted.

Devils Lake became a shipping point for cattlemen. While citizens of the town liked the money that came with the large herds of cattle, and the saloon and brothel owners enjoyed a bonanza, others were not elated with the wild behavior of the cowboys who arrived with the herds. Not content with "painting the town red" in the evening, they would rise early, at least those who were able to, and ride their horses as fast as possible around the "down town" block, shouting and firing their guns into the air, enjoying a "wingding" and "hoorawing" the town, as the saying had it, making sure no slug-a-beds enjoyed their beauty sleep.

Interesting and exciting as were Bartlett, Devils Lake City, and the lake itself, our destination was farther west and north. On June 10th, 1883, we ferried over the Mauvaise Coulee near Churchs Ferry. Mr. Irwin Church, formerly of Northfield, Minnesota, owned the ferry, the only means of crossing. There was a shanty and two large tents on the west bank of the coulee, one of the latter serving as a hotel and other as a store. Mr. Church owned the store; the hotel, consisting of a row of beds on each side with curtains between them and a table in the middle, was owned by Mr. H. O. Orvis. He served meals, too, from a kitchen at the rear of the tent hotel. This was the beginning of what was expected to become a metropolis of the northern plains. Alas, three years later when the Great Northern Railroad was constructed through to the Pacific coast, the right of way missed the potential city, crossing the coulee about a mile north of where it was expected. The station named Churchs Ferry never saw a ferry. At the time of this writing,[40] the coulee has been dry for many years and it requires close inspection to detect the Mauvaise Coulee bed. In all, we drove about forty miles beyond the terminal of the Great Northern Railroad to a point where, according to tentative surveys, the Northern Pacific and the Great Northern tracks would intersect. Our land lay a mile or two north of one lake, according to

Andrew, and west of another near where he expected
a town would soon be located.[41]

      Mr. Church, who had helped Andrew select the land,
drove with us from Churchs Ferry north about ten miles to
our farm and future home. The drive through the spectacular
countryside remains vivid in my memory. There had been
plenty of rain and a great variety of flowers dappling the
luxuriant prairie grass perfumed the air. Meadowlarks and
other birds trilled their music and sunshine seemed unusually
bright, beaming us a warm and friendly welcome. About three
miles north of Churchs Ferry we came to a large lake which
occupied about a quarter of the township and was later named
Lake Irwin in honor of Mr. Irwin Church. We had to drive
around the west side of the lake which was alive with ducks,
geese, and other fowl, welcome supplements to our diet in our
new surroundings.

19

NEW LAND, NEW PROBLEMS, AND A NEW HOME

When we had gone around the west end of the lake, we drove in a northeasterly direction for almost two miles where we came to a slight elevation adorned with a small pile of lumber left there by Andrew on his scouting trip two to three weeks earlier. Stopping our faithful oxen that had brought us to this promised land, he made the long awaited announcement, "Here is our home." Joyfully, we unhitched our beasts of burden and, with the other cattle, turned them loose to eat all they wanted of the lush, wild prairie grass. There was plenty of water in a small depression near where we stretched out on the ground, tired from the long, slow trip but happy and thankful that we had arrived at our destination. We were home and there was nothing to see except the endless prairie, but what a prairie! To the north and west it seemed to sweep on forever. The terrain undulated slightly with no danger of flooding, a primary consideration in our choice of new land.

The site was bordered on the south by the glistening waters of Lake Irwin and on the east by a larger body of water in which there appeared to be an island covered with timber—or perhaps it was merely a knoll covered with brush—and we were the victims of wishful thinking. There was enough indecision about the matter to create some mystery and engender a spirit of adventure that demanded a trip of exploration which we undertook a few days later. If we found trees I was determined to bring home an ample supply of saplings to create a grove around our future house.

The starkness of the plain about us needed to be relieved and, anyway, I missed my old friends and wanted some near me.

Andrew, on his earlier visit, had marked out three quarter sections of land and had left a small stack of lumber on each. Our first order of business, after our brief rest, was to see if the lumber piles were still intact. We found them, but we found something more, less pleasant to contemplate. Somebody had erected three shanties of half-inch lumber, two of them on our land, claiming two of the three quarter sections Andrew had selected. We were surprised and quite unprepared for this development, but upon investigation, we found the shanties unoccupied.

"I was up this way two days ago," said Mr. Church, "and these shanties were not here then. They must have been put up yesterday."

We faced an alarming situation. I don't know what we would have done if Mr. Church had not been with us. Less than a month earlier, the Ward brothers had been shot and killed near Devils Lake because they jumped another man's land, and here we were facing the possibility that someone was claiming two plots that we called ours. On the face of it the situation was ludicrous because there was any amount of the same kind of land as far as the horizon. Why quarrel with anybody about it when so much was available for the taking? But, getting our danders up, we thought our land was just a little better than other parcels, situated with the lakes south and east of us and that mysterious island awaiting exploration. The more we thought about it the more we felt our particular selection was worth a fight to keep it, if need arose.

"If I were you," said Mr. Church, "I'd stick to this spot. It's the finest in the whole coulee country. We'll hitch the oxen to two of these shanties and pull them off your land over to the third, and that will be the beginning of a city. Then put up your own shanties. You were here first and they, whoever they are, are the claim jumpers." He echoed our thoughts.

We acted on Mr. Church's advice and the city was started but it never grew. The shanties were made, as I mentioned earlier, of flimsy, half-inch lumber and were damaged and scattered by fall storms all over the acreage they were meant to hold. But this is getting ahead of my story.

Those who have not experienced pioneering new territory can hardly realize what it means to stop your team and wagon on the naked plains, thirty miles as the crow flies from the nearest town or railroad, with few funds, little fuel, and no financial backing, and try to make a home for yourself and your family. Andrew, Matilda, and I had only ourselves to depend on and sometimes we wondered if all our efforts were really worthwhile. But in our periods of discouragement or depression, one of us would somehow renew our hope and courage and, with our faith in God and ourselves restored, we forged ahead. After all, we had nothing but our time to lose and much to gain. The soil was deep, black loam with clay subsoil, containing just enough sand to keep the plow scoured, and we could have all we wanted merely for the taking.

After Mr. Church, Andrew, and I had grouped the interloper's shanties together it was late afternoon and time to sit down to a meal Matilda had prepared. She was a first-class cook seemingly able to put tasty and nourishing food together from practically nothing. Her culinary skills elicited much praise and thanks from Mr. Church, who, after a bit more conversation, departed on business of his own. We then unloaded the wagon, placing its contents in a compact pile that could be covered by our canvas in the event of rain. The wagon box was made into a bedroom large enough to accommodate all three of us provided the middle one slept end to end. The day, our first on our new land, closed fittingly with a gorgeous sunset that seemed to flood the landscape with its peculiarly friendly glow which dwindled away into darkness. As the long twilight died, our conversation became spasmodic and slowly faded into silence, leaving each of us locked in his or her own thoughts about how far we had come and of those we had left behind in the Red River Valley.

All of us were homesick, I think—at least, I was—lonesome for the other members of our family. But those melancholy thoughts were soon dissolved in sleep that kept our minds and exhausted bodies in thrall until the sun was far above the eastern horizon. We found the cattle peacefully grazing except our excellent milch cow which stood patiently near the wagon waiting to be milked. She had experienced some shrinkage during our western trek, but when she recovered her capacity she was again, to a great extent, our source of food supplies.

After breakfast had been eaten and enjoyed, Andrew and I tackled our most pressing need, that of shelter. We hauled the lumber piles to the site chosen for our house and went to work. We didn't need an architect for what we had in mind; a simple 14' by 16' box-like structure. We had the materials and tools, Andrew had the expertise, and I some experience at building, too. By the evening of the second day we had the walls up and most of the roof in place and finished the house the third day. That amazing speed resulted in a house made of one inch boards with tar paper covering both walls and roof. The tar paper was held in place by laths, fastened with shingle nails, my specialty. The overall result was not very handsome, in fact, the white strips of lath on the black background reminded me of a zebra, but it would serve our needs. We put a door in the middle of the south end and half-windows on the east and west sides. We had only half enough lumber for the floor but used what we did have, put in the stove, converted a dry goods box into a table, and created a cupboard from a couple of smaller boxes. Later on, before winter arrived, we finished the floor.

Matilda was busy cutting and sewing and by the time Andrew and I finished hanging our makeshift cupboards, she had curtains for the half windows ready to hang which, when in place, did wonders in creating a homey appearance and atmosphere. We placed the beds in the half that had no floor, cut some tall grass, and, when it had thoroughly dried, used it to stuff the bed ticks, making quite comfortable beds. We got a fire going in the stove, trooped outside and, as we watched smoke curl from the stovepipe chimney, we sang "Home, Sweet Home."

Our house would have to shelter us from winter's blasts which we knew would be severe. There was no insulation now except the tar paper, against which we would pile sod in the fall, but we would still use prodigious amounts of fuel. We had some wood that we had brought with us or had picked up on our way west, but even using it as sparingly as we could for cooking, our supply was dwindling rapidly. We counted our sticks of firewood and mourned each one's departure as it disappeared into the stove. To stretch the life of our woodpile we gathered buffalo "chips," that is, dried buffalo manure, of which there was a plentiful supply on the surrounding prairie. The chips burned fairly satisfactorily but created an offensive odor, increasing our interest in the mysterious island in the lake to our east.

20

THE ISLAND: FUEL, SAPLINGS, AND FEAR

Driven by curiosity and our need for fuel, Andrew and I tightened our wagon box with cleats, rags, and what not, soaked it thoroughly to shrink the seams and cracks, and thereby made a Mayflower to take us on our voyage of discovery. When we judged the wind to be favorable, we hauled the wagon to the shore, launched our "ship" and, with a blanket for a sail (our canvas was too big) and a spade and shovel for oars, we navigated over the waters of our eastern lake, which, as far as we knew, had no name,[42] to see what was on that intriguing isle.

The trip to our destination was slow. We shipped some water and got our feet wet, but, on the whole, the wagon box proved quite seaworthy and stable. We found our goal to be indeed an island, covered with box elder and cottonwood trees. Great numbers of ducks and other fowl greeted us but we discovered no recent trace of man. We walked around, across, and through it until Andrew called out to me, a little distance from him, to come and see what he'd found. He pointed to some slight depressions and bits of charred wood, indications that people had been there in some remote time before the trees and bushes growing in the depressions had taken root. Perhaps Indians had used it as a safe, moated campground.

Fascinating as were our discoveries, our principal purposes for the boat trip were to find fuel and to secure saplings to plant around our house. We cut down about two wagon loads of portable sized trees, trimmed them, and dragged the trunks to the shore where we fashioned them into a raft. Some were dry and manageable but others were green and heavy and barely floated. When we had our raft finished, we tied it to the wagon box boat, loaded our saplings, and attempted to tow it to the west shore of the lake. We couldn't do it. The west wind that helped us to the island was now against us and we could make no headway. Our solution was to strip off our clothes, get into the lake, and manhandle the raft and boat to the north end of the island where it was only a short distance to the north shore of the lake. We had no idea of the water's depth between the island and the shore but, encountering no drop-off, we kept going and found the lake to be no more than four feet deep.

By then darkness was falling but doggedly we kept westering our precious cargo along the shore until we arrived, we calculated, at our original embarkation point. It was then about three o'clock in the morning. The water was warm but once out of it we hastily dressed to avoid catching a chill, securely tethered the raft and wagon box, and set off to find the oxen and wagon frame. In the dark we could locate neither, but a candle burning in a window guided us to the house where we thought we would get a warm welcome from Matilda. She wasn't there. Alarmed, thoughts of sleep forgotten, we searched everywhere with no success. Fearing the worst, we looked into the shallow well we had dug on the edge of a small marsh, but we found no trace of her. Near despair, we waited for the dawn, and as light increased, Andrew spotted her with the oxen and chassis, at our embarkation point. We had miscalculated in the dark and got out of the water too soon.

Relieved at finding her, we made signals with the lamp, but, with her attention focused on the lake, she couldn't see them. Alternately running and walking, we hastened to her as fast as we could and found her weeping, bedraggled, and exhausted. She had convinced herself we had cap-sized and drowned, and was almost hysterical when we finally reached her. Matilda was so shaken by her fears it took some time for her to regain her composure, but we all enjoyed our mutual relief and happy reunion. Ourselves again, we hitched the oxen to the wagon frame, went over to the raft of logs, hoisted the wagon box into place, loaded some of the logs, and headed home. We were a closer knit family group than ever before. It was a glorious Sunday morning, our first in our new home, made unforgettable by our experiences of the night before and a thanksgiving service we conducted out of doors.

During that week we broke a piece of land near the house to plant the small trees we had brought back from the island, as well as some potatoes. The sod was tough, built up over centuries by the roots of buffalo grass, but by harrowing diligently we managed to pulverize it and planted, in alternate rows, trees and potatoes. We had been told that trees could not be made to grow on the plains but we disproved that rumor. By cultivating them as we did potatoes, they flourished to such an extent neighbors began to call our place "The Forest" and came there to hold family picnics. Encouraged by our success others planted trees around their homes and created many groves in the community.

After living on our farm for about a year we learned from some Indians the name of the lake east of us. They called it "Lac Aux Mortes" in French, translated to "Lake of the Dead" in English, and the island where we cut wood and found saplings they called "Dead Man's Island."[43] At One time, according to the story we were told, a tribe of Indians regularly wintered on the island but one year, long ago, not only did game become scarce but it snowed so heavily it became impossible to hunt. The tribe, faced with starvation, sent a few of the strongest braves to barter for food at Fort Garry, the nearest trading post.[44] It took them about three weeks to make the round trip, we were told, but when they returned with provisions, they found all their friends and relatives dead from cold and starvation. Hence the names of the lake and island. The Indians believe the sounds of the wind in the islands treetops are the spirits of the dead crying for food and shelter.

21

BUFFALO BONES AND CLAIM JUMPERS

In July, 1883, shortly after we had arrived, staked out our claim, and built our house, the Great Northern Railroad's tracks reached the site of the new Devils Lake City. It remained the western terminal of the railroad for three years and during that time, in addition to losing the word City from its name, it became a lively and growing town. Tourists and travelers came and went but many stayed, causing a flurry of building activity. Needing every dime we could lay our hands on, it was decided among the three of us that Andrew should go there, hire out his carpentry skills, and make as much money as he could while Matilda and I would remain on the claim. Until we brought in a crop, we had to utilize every expedient possible and, because I was eighteen years old, strong and healthy as a horse, we all agreed Andrew could safely leave without worrying about us. While he was gone I would break up all the land time would allow. The oxen were well-fed and healthy, there had been plenty of rainfall, and the prairie was in excellent condition for plowing. Andrew left for Devils Lake immediately our decision was made and I set to work on the land.

I laid out a furrow a mile long covering two quarter sections. As a rule I plowed four rounds in the forenoon and four again in the afternoon, working the oxen and myself sixteen miles per day, about all that the oxen could manage. If the weather was very hot I started work at five o'clock in the morning and worked until about ten, let the oxen feed and rest until three o'clock in the afternoon and then would plow until near dark. That schedule kept the animals in good condition (as well as myself) and I believe they did more work than if I had driven them during the hottest part of the day. Sticking to this routine, I broke up 35 acres. It was hard work but on the whole I enjoyed following the plow and inhaling the sweet scents that rose from newly turned earth.

We discovered there was a market for buffalo bones. What was done with them I do not know,[45] but around us on the prairie were a great number of scattered bones, partial and whole skeletons of bison. We gathered a large pile of them, many from the land I plowed, which later in the fall we hauled to Devils Lake and sold for $12.00 per ton, a very welcome addition to our money cache. The skulls with horns intact were put aside and, in our spare time, we cleaned, polished, mounted, and readied them for sale. The horns were black as ebony, took a high polish, were an attractive ornament, and sold for as much as $5.00 a pair to tourists who came to Devils Lake to see the West and all its wonders.

One day as I was plowing I saw two men coming in my direction. One carried a shotgun and the other a saw and hammer. Boldly they came up to me as I brought the oxen to a halt.

"Who moved our shanties?" asked the taller man with the gun.

"We did."

"Don't you know it's a state prison offense to molest other people's property?"

"Well," I said, "We're not in a state and there's no prison, but that's beside the point. You built shanties on our land, not the other way around."

"It's not your land!" he said.

"When you built your shanties, didn't you see the corner rods, the furrows around the land, and the piles of lumber on it?"

"They weren't there when we built our shanties," he came back.

"That's right! They weren't there," joined in the man with the hammer and saw, adding a string of profanity to reinforce his words.

As I listened to their bluster, sized up their ragged clothes, the absence of oxen, wagon, and equipment, I realized they were bluffing, that they had no intentions of developing the land.

"We know for a fact you built those shanties the day before we returned to our claim and we can prove it. Mr. Church will attest to that fact. What's more, the corners were marked and the furrows plowed at least two weeks before we came to settle. Now, if you'll get out of my way I have work to do," I said, getting the oxen moving.

"We have selected this land and we propose to have it," flung back the man with the gun, "and if you know what's healthy for you, you'd better pull right out of here. We've got guns and by God we're not afraid to use them!"

I stopped the oxen that had barely started moving the plow, turned to them and, speaking more bravely than I felt, said, "Two can play at that game. We have shooting irons too, and if you want a showdown you can have it."

They said nothing.

"Now, I'm going to plow. I haven't got the time to fool around talking to you." I started the oxen moving, put my weight on the plow, and left them to themselves. They sat down on the prairie for a while and then rose and walked over toward their shanties. I had put up a bold front and called their bluff but the reaction left me a bit shaken, so I turned loose the oxen and went into the house. I did not intend to tell Matilda anything about what had occurred for fear she would be frightened but it was an unusual time to quit work. She remarked on that fact, noticed how pale I was, and concluded I was sick. I wasn't, but I had to satisfy her curiosity. Holding nothing back, I told her of the encounter with the claim jumpers. She was surprised and alarmed but after a more or less cool discussion, we decided to stay in the house and await the next move of the enemy. Let them think we were preparing to defend ourselves against an attack. Meanwhile we commended ourselves to God and invoked his protection.

We waited. Nothing happened. That night my sister did not sleep well. She heard, or thought she heard, voices and odd noises periodically. She woke me once, but hearing nothing, I calmed her and then returned to my dreams, fortunate in sleeping well even under those circumstances. Contributing to her disquiet and to the unpleasantness of the situation was our awareness of the recent shootings of claim jumpers near Devils Lake. We knew we were in the right regarding our land, but a stranger with a gun can behave unpredictably. We would see if my response to their highhanded demands had been the correct course to take.

Evidently it did the trick. In the morning the pair of men were not visible and, mustering our courage, Matilda and I walked over to their shanties, but found them empty. Feeling much better, we settled into our daily work and the men were soon forgotten. They never reappeared or troubled us again. During the fall the shanties blew down and the next spring we gathered up and disposed of the wreckage. Later, when the land was surveyed and came on the market, we filed on that quarter section too. We never heard who they were, whence they came, or what happened to them but we thank them for injecting a bit of drama and excitement into our lives.

When I had plowed the 35 acres that was my goal, Matilda, Andrew, and I discussed, during one of his visits from Devils Lake, what crops we should sow. We calculated that many others, probably with horses, would come to our part of the country the following spring and summer and would require oats for feed and seed wheat to plant. By the time the acreage was plowed, the growing period was upon us and we hurriedly sowed 30 acres in oats and 5 acres in wheat. Later we harvested a good crop of oats and a fairly bountiful supply of wheat. During the winter, after the family was reunited, we handpicked the wheat clean of foul seeds when we weren't busy cleaning, polishing, and mounting buffalo horns.

Getting ahead of my narrative a bit, events turned out pretty much as we expected. The next growing season (1884) we produced a fine crop of clean wheat. Word spread among newcomers to the area that oats and seed wheat were available at our farm and we sold as much of both as we could spare, saving us the time and effort required to haul our products to Devils Lake, 25 miles away. We could have sold much more to eager buyers, some of whom came great distances to secure supplies. We regretted we had not broken more ground the first year but, as I have explained, with all the other tasks necessary to do to prepare for our first winter, 35 acres of plowing was all I could manage. The drudgery of hand picking our first wheat crop resulted in harvests of exceptionally clean wheat much in demand as seed for many years.

22

FAMILY UNITED AND FARM COMPLETED

Toward the end of summer, 1883, Andrew drove back to the Red River Valley to bring the rest of the family, the remainder of our household goods and cattle to our new home. Johanna, now fifteen years old, and Nils, twelve, stayed behind to care for the livestock while Andrew took my parents to Grand Forks and put them on a train. He hurried back to the youngsters, loaded the wagon, and brought them and the cattle more leisurely to the new farm. In the meantime, knowing when my parents would arrive, I met their train at Devils Lake with a neighbor's oxen and rig and brought them home. Mother was not well and traveled reclining on a cot, which was a damper on the joy of our reunion. Both of my parents, nevertheless, were delighted to have left behind the Red River mud, the tall grass, the mosquitoes, and the danger of probable floods every spring, and were looking forward eagerly to a new farm and a better opportunity.

Ever since their arrival in America in 1866, my parents, especially my mother, unrelentingly had sought a farm. Undismayed by our false start near the Red River, she was looking forward to the realization of her hopes and dreams after seventeen years of frustration in the new world. She had experienced disappointment and adversity, and with my semi-invalided father to care for and all us children to support and raise, she had carried a load that was enough to crush most women.

When they came to Ramsey County, Dakota Territory to live, my father Johan was just turning 64, having been born September 11th, 1819 and my mother Nicoline would shortly be 56, with her birth date September 29th, 1827. They were married on January 4th, 1847. Father was about 5 feet 10 or 11 inches in height and was fairly slim. He had been trained to be a teacher as well as an accountant, but his ambition had been to own and operate a bookstore in Bergen, Norway. He worked as both a teacher and bookkeeper until he had enough money saved to realize his ambition when he was stricken with typhoid fever, hospitalized for six months, and nearly died. That illness may have accounted for his weakness and frail health that plagued him the rest of his long life. A student and bibliophile by nature, given to intellectual pursuits rather than physical, he was ill-suited to be a pioneer farmer in a new land. I've often thought he must have wondered to himself why and what he was doing here in America, trying to be something he knew in his heart he could never be, with frail health and advancing age against him, especially in raw country such as Dakota Territory.

Mother, although nearly 56, seemed much younger to me than Father, whom I always thought of as an old man. She had dark brown hair, small feet, and beautiful tapering fingers. She was 5 feet 9 inches tall and weighed 140 pounds in her prime. She was dignified, commanding, and attractive. Her eyes were very expressive and when she was young she must have been beautiful. She was honest and dependable, a good conversationalist, possessed a keen intellect, and was most persuasive and articulate. .

Whereas Father, as a boy, had been spoiled and pampered by an indulgent family, my mother sprang from strong, intelligent country stock in Norway, the daughter of my remarkable grandfather, Anders Buvarp. My mother was practical and down to earth while Father was totally wooden handed when it came to any kind of manual work. Or he may have thought that sort of thing was beneath him. At any rate, I believe my mother soon realized it was up to her to provide whatever was needed by the family, and she bore that burden indefatigably. Nothing was impossible to that indomitable woman. She was positive, optimistic, and fiercely ambitious for her children. She always resented the idea that any of us should work under a boss; we should work for ourselves and to do that we should be as highly educated as possible. On the way home from Devils Lake she again brought the matter up and urged me not to forget my original ambition and to go back to school.

Along the way we stopped to give the oxen a chance to rest and satisfy their hunger on the prairie grass. I brought out a can of pear sauce that I had been holding back, which I knew both my parents enjoyed, and that we shared as our luncheon dessert. I remember as we were taking our ease that I told them that I had been hoping to get back to school but that lately I had about given up my plans in that regard because we were continually moving farther away from schools, I was getting too old to start again, and, anyway, there would be much work in establishing a new home here on the prairie. Not only were my prospects dimming, I told them, but I had observed many people who managed to make their way through life without any education.

It was obvious neither parent was happy with my words so I tried to comfort them (and myself) by saying that I knew of men with education who were not doing as well as some without. Of course, I was rationalizing, talking against my own convictions, trying to fool myself and them, too. No matter how much I talked in that vein, the old longing for an education returned considerably strengthened. They saw through my words, and as we continued our journey, Mother ventured the suggestion of using and improving the land, of which we now had so much, to enable me to return to school. She enjoined me to maintain my resolve, to never value land over education, and not to worry over my advancing age. There would be time, she assured me. I have always valued her sage advice.

It was late when we arrived home to be greeted happily by Matilda. The next morning my parents were all eyes. Mother had been less than rapturous about the prairie as we came from Devils Lake, but she felt better about it after a night's rest. Father walked around the farm and expressed his joy and satisfaction over the location, the lay of the land, the excellent quality and drainage of the soil, the plowed 35 acres, and the tree and potato plantings. A few days later, when

Andrew, Josie, and Nils arrived with the cattle and goods, we were all together and life seemed more like living again.

I had become quite a proficient plowman. I enjoyed seeing the furrows lie in regular, flat rows with all grass covered. I took plenty of time to keep the plowshares sharp so as to cut the sod cleanly, leaving nothing uncut between the furrows. Andrew and I agreed the 35 acres I had broken were enough—we wouldn't have time to do more that year. Breaking the land means plowing about two inches deep. That I had done, but now we had to backset it, which means plowing it back again two inches deeper so as to get about two inches of subsoil on top of the sod.

In addition to preparing the land for seeding, we had to build a stable, which we made of sod, and provision it with a winter's supply of hay. There was a plentiful crop of tall grass growing in low places on the prairie that we cut, stacked, and dried. Another job facing Andrew and me was to dig a new well. Our first was dug near a small marsh, and although it was deep, we were rewarded with very little water. Luckily, one day two Indians[46] stopped at the farm to get a drink. They told us we should dig a well on higher ground where there were indications of the presence of a badger colony. Badgers knew, the Indians told us, where water could be found and build their homes near or on top of the water source, then dig in a spiral pattern down to it. We dug where our native friends told us to and encountered the badger spiral. We followed it down and found abundant clear and good tasting water. (Five years later we built a larger, permanent house near that well.) In addition, we had to sod up the house for winter and haul home as much wood as we could from Devils Lake. All in all we had perhaps more than we could hope to accomplish before the advent of cold weather. We were all keenly aware of what winter meant in that latitude.

Of the jobs facing us that fall we chose first to cut and stack our hay before building the stable. When we had a plentiful supply for the winter ahead, we went after sod. As I mentioned earlier, prairie sod was very tough and hard to work with. We cut it up in eighteen inch lengths and, laying them as one would blocks or bricks, built the walls of the stable. Next, we needed "crutches" to act as pillars to hold a center beam that, in turn, would support the roof. "Crutches" were stout, long stringers branching in two at the top to form a "Y," much like a very long handled slingshot. To get them, as well as the center beam and the roof railings, we had to make a trip to the shore of Devils Lake. We knew of a large tract of timber controlled by a man who was half Sioux Indian who sold it off at $1.00 per load regardless of the load's size.

After we made arrangements with the owner of the timber tract, Andrew and I loaded our wagon with a fair number of stringers and railings, anticipating little trouble getting it home. We planned to stay overnight and leave in the morning, but during the night it started to rain with no letup until morning, thoroughly soaking the road. We knew the oxen could not pull our load through the mire, off-loaded about a quarter of the freight, got the oxen moving, very slowly, until they bogged down. We had to off-load about another quarter of the initial weight and finally, laboriously, reached home with half of our original load. We went back the next day and retrieved our discarded crutches and stringers, but that trip remains nightmarishly in my memory. By the time we finished we knew intimately, from so much handling, each crutch and railing that went into the construction of our stable.

We trimmed our crutches to uniform length, set them in place, used a couple or three of the heaviest rails to form a beam which we placed in the "Y"s, and then laid one end of the rails on the sod wall and the other on the beam. We cut willows we found near Lake Irwin, laid them on the roof rails, and over the willows put a thick layer of the coarsest hay we could find. This systematic procedure created an amazingly efficient roof. The covering had enough time before winter arrived to settle and compact, which insured a warm stable during the cold weather season.[47]

To survive the coming icy blasts, we had to protect ourselves at least as well as we had the animals. The house walls, one thickness of lumber covered with tarpaper, had to be insulated. Once more to the sod pits! We piled sod about six inches from the walls, filled the air space with dirt, and as we went up to the eaves left less and less space, in effect, tapering the walls and giving them strength. It was comforting to know we would be as cozy as our cattle—well, almost, anyway, since we were bound to lose heat through our un-sodded roof.

Knowing we were going to need a lot of fuel and also realizing there would be a great demand for firewood the next year as the area became settled, we hauled all the wood we possibly could after the ground froze. At a place called Graham's Island near Devils Lake we found a source of ash trees which make excellent firewood. By leaving home early, before daylight, we arrived at our destination by early afternoon, leaving us enough time to fell the trees, trim the branches, and be ready for loading the wagon the next morning.

As a rule the load was heavy, the road rough (but not muddy), and often we saw the sun set while we were still ten or twelve miles from home, but a lantern placed on a high pole near our house guided us to our farmyard. One such night a strong wind extinguished the light and we missed home by about a mile. The oxen, plodding on, stumbled into a plowed area. We stopped, examined the furrows, recognized our handiwork, placed the field in our mental maps, and went unerringly home. In such flat, monotonous country, even a piece of plowing seemed like a sociable, old friend. The result of our, seemingly, unremitting toil was a wood pile that lasted over two years.

23

LAND LAWS, LAND FILING, AND LAND FEVER

When we came to Dakota Territory to make a home, the land had not yet been surveyed. As I indicated earlier in this narrative, the only way we could designate our land was to put in corner rods or stakes and plow a furrow or two around it. We had no way of measuring the exact distances but paced it out at seven steps to the rod, (a rod is sixteen feet,) and then added a pace or two or three for good measure, making sure the quarter sections were as close to 160 acres as possible.

In the fall of 1883 we saw some surveyors run an east-west line, setting section and quarter section markers. We had to find out what all the activity was about. One member of the crew explained that the line they were running was the 22nd standard parallel,[48] that the section and quarter section markers they were setting applied to the township north of us and that our township would be surveyed from the south. He also told us the 22nd standard parallel would be the dividing line between Ramsey County in which our land was located and Towner County north of us. We found out that when our township was surveyed from the south, there would be a slight jog between the lines north and south of the parallel due to the curvature of the earth. The jog turned out to be about twenty rods, and accounts for the short crooks every six miles in roads running north and south,[49] and similar compensating jogs in north-south boundary lines of counties. A few days later another surveying crew ran lines and established the corners of our land. Not too surprisingly, our generously paced-out measurements were in error and our two quarter sections, to our delight, turned out to be officially three.

At that time government land could be secured under three different laws. According to the Pre-emption Law, a person could take 160 acres, i.e., a quarter section, live on it six months, make certain improvements and then acquire it by paying $200.00. At the same time he or she could file on 160 acres under the Tree Planting Law. According to its provisions, he or she had to plant ten acres in trees and have a stipulated number of them flourishing at the end of five years. Lastly, one could file under the Homestead Act of 1862 on another 160 acres, obtain title by improving the land and making it his or her home for five years. By those three methods, then, it was possible for anyone of age (21) to acquire ownership of three quarter sections, i.e., 480 acres of land.

When the government survey was completed and our land lines adjusted, we found that Andrew and my father each had a half section, 320 acres, and Matilda a quarter section. Later she took a tree claim adjoining her land to the west that gave us a total of 960 acres in one piece. Andrew had used up his Homestead rights in the Red River Valley and had to acquire his land by means of a Pre-emption and a Tree claim, Father his by a Homestead and a Tree claim, and Matilda's first quarter section was obtained by Pre-emption.

In 1886, when I turned 21, I also took a Pre-emption and a Tree claim, increasing our land holdings to 1,280 acres. All the land the two would-be claim jumpers had deserted was included in our holdings. Earlier, I described our success in planting trees, but we changed our procedure on our Tree Planting claims. We broke the land the first year, sowed wheat the second, plowed extra deep and planted trees the third, cultivated them as we did corn, and they flourished. Fortunately, we enjoyed plenty of rainfall during our first two years, an ingredient indispensable for tree culture.

There is no doubt all of us were victims of land fever. Unable to file in the fall of 1883 because I was too young, I nevertheless built a sod shanty on a quarter section I coveted. It was distinguished by a slight elevation pretty well covered with stones. I kept the knoll burned off and all the rocks exposed to view as a deterrent to anyone else who might take an interest in claiming it. There was any amount of fine land elsewhere that could be had for the taking and my little patch was passed over. My ruse worked and saved the land for me over a period of two and a half years. I was eager to have that particular acreage because it adjoined our holdings. Alas! Despite my ruses, plans, and tricks, only a month before my 21st birthday that parcel of land was claimed by somebody else and my hopes went glimmering.

Word spread through the community that the government intended to establish a land filing office in Devils Lake and a specified date was set when it would open for business. Everyone was eager to legitimize his or her land holdings and great excitement was generated as the anticipated day approached. People left for town in plenty of time, some, who lived at a distance, started two or three days in advance. Some folks pooled their resources, as many as twelve traveled in one conveyance and camped out in tents or in their prairie schooners, determined to reach the land office before someone else filed on their claims.

On the designated day, despite the cold weather, would-be filers began forming a group as early as 5:00 A.M. although the office would not open its doors until 9:00. By the latter hour the street in front of the office was packed—everybody attempted to crowd as close to the office doors as possible and gave off a cloud of vapor from their breath and body heat in the sub-zero weather. Some who had arrived very early were exhausted from cold and fatigue. I heard some unprintable language uttered and saw some women faint in the press of people. Anyone who has not gone through a land filing rush can have no idea of the near hysteria that rules the crowd. Several extra officers were on hand to keep order, which proved a wise precaution, and prevented trampling and possible injury. There were numbers of women in the crowd who were thankful indeed for the protection.

When the doors opened, there was an immediate crush at the counters but order was soon restored. Wisely, the authorities in charge of the office provided extra clerks to serve the applicants which hastened the processing of claims. The crowd was so large, however, that, even with the clerks working speedily and efficiently, some did not get their filing papers until late in the afternoon. Excited worry proved unfounded as the land office abided strictly by the rules: the person who had lived on, or made improvements on, a quarter section, had his claim honored, even if someone else was ahead of him in the lines. There were a few contests primarily because when the land was surveyed, two neighbors found they were living on the same quarter section. All altercations of that nature were settled without bloodshed.

Looking back on that wild day I have nothing but admiration for the skill and patience of the officers and personnel who created order from the chaotic conditions that prevailed in the street. No doubt those in charge had experienced similar situations and were familiar with how to proceed fairly and tame a mob of land seekers. They knew how to handle "land office" business to nearly everyone's satisfaction. It was a great relief to members of my family when they were finished filing and knew, indisputably, that they then owned their land.

About a mile and a half west of us was a rather high ridge beyond which a Mr. Walker had settled. A former wheat speculator from Illinois, he arrived with a great deal of farm machinery and a large herd of cattle. We did not know about him or he about us for some time after he took possession of his holdings. He gained a great deal of land by having his employees file, prove it up, and then turn it over to him.

After I had lost my coveted, stone-covered quarter section, just a month before I turned 21, as I've mentioned earlier, I chose another 160 acre parcel contiguous with Andrew's tree claim and immediately began plowing. As I was working, Mr. Walker and one of his men approached me. I halted the oxen as they neared and we talked very sociably. From the drift of the conversation I realized Mr. Walker wanted the land but assumed, since I was plowing, it was already mine.

I did not disillusion him but, as soon as I was of age, I filed a pre-emption claim.

I also wanted a tree claim but the law allowed no more than one per section of land. A man named Olaf Berg had filed on a tree claim east of Andrew's holdings in another section but was not living up to the law, thus forfeiting his right to it. He had moved away after plowing only a portion of the required number of acres. I discovered his address, wrote, and offered him $50.00 for the relinquishment of his claim. He wrote back demanding $100.00. The land could be taken from him by default, but that could entail a troublesome procedure which I preferred to avoid.

Shortly after my correspondence exchange with Mr. Berg, and while Andrew and I were planting trees on his claim, we saw Walker and one of his friends, Mr. Corduck, running lines and measuring the amount of plowed soil on Mr. Berg's land. Both of us knew what that meant. Andrew told me if I wanted that tree claim I'd better get to the land office by morning. I stopped work, went to the house, changed clothes, and started to hike to Churchs Ferry, ten miles away. As bad luck would have it, I met one of Walker's men with a load of lumber, who stopped his team and insisted on chatting a bit, giving me a good looking over while we talked. When I reached Churchs Ferry I learned a construction train would make a run from the railhead, now at Churchs Ferry, to Devils Lake at 9 o'clock the next morning. With the coming of the railroad, Mr. Orvis, who had begun business in a tent near Mauvaise Coulee, had built a hotel, The Orvis House, in the transplanted, rapidly growing town. Matilda had taken a job as a cook in the new establishment and I stayed with her over night.

The next morning, bright and early, I boarded the train but about twenty minutes before departure I saw Walker and Corduck approaching in a wagon. Sizing up the odds and not knowing how they would react if they spotted me, I chose discretion over valor and slipped into the toilet of the caboose. They stopped near the train, Walker dismounted, walked through the caboose, and back to the wagon. I heard him say, in response to Corduck's query, "No, he ain't there," and

was relieved to see them drive off in the direction of Devils
Lake. Evidently Walker's man, whom I had met on the road,
had reported he had seen me dressed in my Sunday best, and
Walker, immediately surmising my destination and intent, had
started in pursuit.

Impatient, I thought the train would never start but it
did in good time and when we reached Devils Lake, I hurried
to the land office and filed a contest on Mr. Berg's tree claim.
While I was about my business, which took some little time,
the train was loaded with ties and rails and was ready to return
to Churchs Ferry when I finished. The timing was perfect,
almost as if the Great Northern train crew knew and approved
of my activity. I regained my place in the caboose and as we
left Devils Lake I saw Walker and Corduck arrive. Later I
learned they were extremely irate when told I had beat them
to it. Mr. Walker was given to profanity, I discovered, for
according to reports the air turned blue from his remarks about
that stupid, red headed, snot nosed, Norwegian kid who had
beat him at his own game. As a result of my contest of Mr.
Berg's claim, a trial was held about a month later. He did not
appear and thus forfeited his rights to the land. The tree claim
was mine.

24

THE LIGHTER SIDE OF LIFE ON THE PLAINS

Looking back to those early days on the prairie, most memories are associated with hard work and the difficulties of making a new life, but, occasionally, there was time for gatherings, bees of one kind or another, picnics, and parties among neighbors. We had occasion for laughter, too, at some of the foolishness and foibles of people we knew. One of the jokes of the time involved the Broody brothers, who had opened a store and developed a large trade in Devils Lake. If they had sold out of a particular item requested by a customer, one or the other would say, "We're all out, but we have a carload on the way." One day a wag entered the Broody Brothers emporium and, straightfaced, asked for a dozen postholes. Without batting an eye, one of the brothers gave the usual response. Other customers in the store overheard the exchange and it became one of the great jokes of the community. The Broodys were clever men who encouraged the fun at their expense, turning the joke into a publicity stunt that kept the name of their establishment in people's minds. The phrase became a kind of slogan that brought many customers to their place of business.

As we had expected, there was a sizable influx of newcomers to the area in the spring and summer of 1884 who came both by train and covered wagon. A "Mutt and Jeff"[50] pair of men, named Big Dan and Little Ike, did a thriving business "selling" claims to the gullible tenderfeet who wandered into their clutches. Their skin game was simplicity itself. They put a shanty on a piece of land in which Little Ike lived while his partner found eager buyers in Devils Lake, offering to locate them on some fine land with prime growing possibilities. Many were glad to enlist his help and would accompany Big Dan out to the shack to meet his friend Ike and make a deal with him. But Little Ike was reluctant to meet the prospective buyer, reluctant to emerge from his abode. Finally, coaxed outside, Ike would say something like, "Well, this is a fine piece of land and I really want to stay on it." Playing hard to get, Ike would be adamant in resisting the blandishments of Big Dan and the buyer but at the same time he would extol the attractive features of his claim.

When the pair of sharks had the buyer hooked, Big Dan would draw the "sucker" aside and confide his secret knowledge about Little Ike's financial condition, that he knew the little fellow was really hard up, and urge his mark to increase his offer and that might persuade Ike to sell his precious land. When that was done, Little Ike finally would be prevailed upon to sell to the eager purchaser, uttering protestations such as "If I wasn't so hard up I wouldn't sell" and "I'll look for but I know I won't find as good a piece of land as this." Deal completed and cash (always cash) paid to Little Ike, the shanty was moved to another place and the process was repeated with some other tenderfoot. Occasionally their greed overcame their sense and the pair sold the same land to several different buyers and when the shanty was removed, it was next to impossible to know what land belonged to whom. The two confidence men kept their swindles going until so many irate "customers" were after them they found it wise to move to parts unknown to avoid an unpleasant "necktie" party.

One day in the summer of 1884, our place was invaded by a train of mud covered wagons drawn by mules. The people, who came from Missouri and called each other by such names as Priest, Parsons, and Pew, (a leg pulling exercise, I'm sure) had been directed to us in their need for oats, and bought much of our supply. They seemed to have plenty of money, had Negroes with them, and were looking for a place to settle. After they loaded their purchases and had rested a while, they moved on toward the north. Later we learned that this group of families discovered a likely place to stay and, in defiance of others who discouraged them, named the site Cando, just to prove their detractors wrong. The founders of the town were right, for Cando grew and became the county seat of Towner County. Another town, named Willdo, was founded a few miles east of Cando and for some time a sharp competition existed between them but ultimately Cando became the largest town in that part of the Territory and Willdo faded from the map. The Missourians occupied a great deal of land and farmed on an extensive scale. I never discovered if their "churchly" names were real or not.

Al Sather and his brother, Nils, settled about two miles north-west of us, and lived in a 14' by 16' shanty. They shared their quarters during the winter with two bachelor neighbors for reasons of economy and sociability. With four large men sharing such small space, things got quite crowded, forcing a few expedient measures such as using the flour barrel as a table base, and a double-decker bed for the two sojourning bachelors. The sociability usually involved card playing around the flour barrel cum table and heavy smoking by three of the four. The first two losers at cards each day were responsible, in order of their elimination from the game, for preparing the next day's meals and washing and drying the dishes. Two of the four seemed constantly at these tasks, which led me to think a little friendly cheating was going on.

When I visited the Sather place, which I did occasionally, and came to know all four of its residents, I was usually bothered by the heavy tobacco smoke that hung in the air. One of the neighbors, a very tall man, was the only non-smoker of the four and was constantly complaining and standing up, trying to avoid the fumes, but the others paid him no attention. He was tempted, I think, and often threatened, to punch a hole in the roof which was not far above his head but he never did, merely lapsing back into unheeded complaint.

One night late in the fall but before the neighbors moved in for the winter, I stayed all night with the Sathers, sleeping in the upper bunk. When we awoke in the morning we found the floor covered with men from the Missouri settlement, most of them more or less intoxicated. They had unhitched their teams, tied them to their wagons, and then came in and found space on the floor. That was a new experience for me but the Sathers told me it happened quite frequently. Nobody locked their doors in the evening and if anybody needed shelter from the weather or lodgings at night they were always welcome.

We were fortunate in owning three cows that we had brought with us from the Red River Valley farm. Mother always maintained that a cow and a few laying hens furnished half of our necessary victuals but three cows and a henhouse full of chickens could be the foundation of a business. She was skillful and knowing when it came to dairying, having been trained as a child in Norway, and made delicious butter and cheese. Many of the settlers in our proximity were bachelors of both sexes including no less than six girls, at one time, who lived quite near us creating a large and ready market for all the milk, butter, cheese, and eggs that we could spare. I don't know when those young ladies proved up their claims for they seemed to spend more time at our place than they did in their own shanties.

We owned a swift pair of steers that I had half-broken for light driving and called them our buggy team when hitched to a two wheeled cart that substituted for a buggy. One warm afternoon in the summer of 1885, I was going somewhere on an errand and invited the girls, again visiting our place, to go along for the ride. With little hesitation four of them climbed aboard and, the conveyance somewhat crowded, we took off down the rough, rutted track of a road toward Devils Lake. Chatting and giggling, the young ladies and I were enjoying our outing until we came near a buffalo wallow, a large depression with a small boulder in the middle of it. The bison had used the rock as a rubbing post and created the wallow by pawing up the ground around it. We had had recent rains and the depression was full of water, an irresistible attraction for my insufficiently trained oxen. Ignoring my shouted commands and the restraining reins, they raced for the wallow and plunged into the water. Before I could stop them, one of the cart wheels ran up and over the stone, tipping the shrieking girls into the water, giving them an unexpected, involuntary bath.

There was much screaming, cries of surprise and dismay that turned to outrage and indignation when the four wet, muddy, and bedraggled young women realized I had hung on to the wagon and escaped a soaking. If they had taken concerted action against me at that moment I could not have avoided an ignominious fate, but, instead, one of the girls started laughing at the appearance of the others, good nature prevailed, and soon all were appreciating the ridiculousness of the situation. After extricating the team and two-wheeler from the wallow, the girls, somewhat reluctantly, regained their places and, errand postponed, we returned home where the young ladies hurriedly dispersed to their own places to change clothes. I ran into one of my passengers some years later in Northfield who did not forget to mention that fateful cart ride and wholly unanticipated bath.

25

A FOE AND A FRIEND

Just north of Lake of the Dead were several sections of low land covered with a luxuriant growth of grass, used, early on, as a common haying ground by our neighbors and ourselves. When someone mowed around a part of the meadow he was left in possession of the grass in his enclosure, without squabble, out of respect. That procedure was honored as long as there was plenty of grass, but, one hot, dry year the grass was less plentiful and then it was every man for himself. By that time, too, much of the meadow had claims filed on it, further cutting down the grass supply. By keeping an accurate record of all land filed on near us, we knew our neighbor, Mr. Walker, claimed, or had one of his men file, on a quarter section bordering the west shore of the lake, yet again reducing the common ground.

Andrew and I kept our eyes on about forty acres of land that had previously been under water and that was producing good grass. When the soil was firm enough to bear the weight of our oxen, we started to cut the crop with two mowers. Walker, shortly realizing we were mowing on government land, sent one of his men to Devils Lake to file a claim on the parcel. The next day the agent returned, but instead of going south and west of Lake of the Dead he came around the north end from the east. He encountered us before he reported to Walker, and told us he had filed on and now owned the land. We had an extended conversation with him, pointed out his need for a home, and made an offer to swap him a shanty we had available for the grass on his land. Unaware, evidently, that Walker wanted the hay, he readily assented to the deal. We agreed, in turn, to haul the shanty onto the forty acres the next day. We later heard that when he reported his deal to Walker he was treated to a torrent of vituperation for letting us have the grass. We honored our part of the agreement and moved the shanty to the forty acre plot the next day. I admit there was a touch of deception in our dealings with the agent but, as I mentioned earlier, it was every man for himself and, besides, we couldn't let Walker have everything his way.

Mr. Walker, our irascible, wealthy neighbor, had an insatiable lust for land, and used anybody and everybody he could hire to file claims and prove up his acquisition of quarter sections. By 1885 Walker had possession of more than two thousand acres and was looking for more. Where he found his minions was anybody's guess but I think in the saloons and brothels of Devils Lake—drifters, drunks, and ne'er-do-wells, replacements for some of the men who had come with him to the Territory but had moved on. For board, room, and a pittance these derelicts would move onto a piece of land Walker wanted, live in a shanty the required length of time, sworn to by a witness, claim the land, and then sell it to Mr. Walker for a negligible sum.

Walker, a good judge of men, usually had it his way and got what he wanted. But once in a while he made a mistake. One of his men, Tom Hildebrand, not as feckless as the others, proved less malleable to Mr. Walker's schemes and designs. Tom, a blond, tall, young man with sharp blue eyes, and sporting the fashionable handlebar mustache, fetched the mail for the Walker enclave and I got to be a friend of his. (In February, 1885, our farm became a town named Kildahl with a post office. Details of that development are included in the next chapter.) Good natured and talkative, Tom let me know that he knew exactly what was going on, said he was willing to do a job of claiming for Mr. Walker simply because, in a weak moment, he had given his word, but, he made clear to me, he didn't like the man. Tom was living on a quarter section, at least he slept in his shanty, and wanted me to stay with him occasionally and thereby be a witness when it came time to prove up his claim.

I usually took my young brother, Nils, along on these excursions. Going on 14, and having read, I'm sure, one or two of Ned Buntline's dime novels dealing with the wicked, wild, exciting west and its romantic heroes and notorious outlaws, Nils was fascinated with Tom. Although the latter wore neither star nor six-shooter, I'm sure Nils added, in his mind's eye, those embellishments to the person of Tom. Nils had fallen in love with a fictional west, enhanced by the manner and style, the words and entrancing adventures of Tom. The next year we would learn the extent of Nils's enchantment with all things western.

One night in February, 1885, Tom asked us to stay with him once again. His shanty, a little larger than usual, had two double bunks that provided plenty of sleeping space. Snow was blowing, driven by stiff winds, and unable to sleep, we talked and talked. Nils, wide eyed, drank it all in until we retired, quite late. As a result we slept well into the next morning, but when we awoke it was still dark so we remained in our bunks and talked some more. Tom had traveled a great deal, was a skilled storyteller, and described the many places he had seen and the adventures he had experienced. Whether everything he related was true I do not know but he wove an enthralling tale.

Emerging from my trance I realized, suddenly, that the shanty was snowed under. Tom got up, lighted the lamp and found it was about four o'clock. He got the door open a crack, informed us it was just coming daylight, closed it, made a fire, and returned to bed while we continued our conversation for another hour or more. When we got out of bed, dressed, and took a look outdoors again, we found it to be pitch black night. We realized Tom had mistaken the grayness of dusk for dawn, and somehow we had lost twelve hours. I hoped our parents weren't worrying too much about us, but there was nothing to be done except have a meal and go to bed again for another night.

Somewhat ruefully, Nils and I trudged home the next morning after clawing our way out of the huge drift that had enveloped Tom's shanty. Mother and Father were a bit upset but had assumed we had remained at Tom's place, out of the cold. After all, Nils and I had had experience with winter on those northern plains and were well acquainted with the dangers it presented. Still bemused by the loss of a day in my life, I had no trouble testifying that Mr. Tom Hildebrand had indeed slept on his land.

Predictably, Tom and Mr. Walker had a falling out and the latter did not get Hildebrand's land. After proving up his claim, he left the community, no doubt hurried on his way by Walker. Almost two years later, out of the blue, we received a letter from Tom, telling us he was in some sort of financial trouble and offering us his land for a reasonable price. Ideally located for our needs on the shore of Lake of the Dead, including the beach where we landed our raft of firewood taken from Dead Man's Island on our memorable expedition, Andrew bought it. Well grassed, we fenced it, and used it as pasture for our young stock. After the transaction was completed, we never heard from Tom again, to my regret, for he was a real man and would have proved, I'm sure, a valued friend.

Kildahl, Dakota Territory
Postmark.

26

KILDAHL P.O., BRIDES, AND A BABY

Civilization had been left behind when Andrew, Matilda, and I, the first people to settle on land north of Churchs Ferry, arrived in June, 1883. Within a year and a half we had more than enough neighbors to petition Washington for a post office. With all the coming and going on our place by customers for firewood, oats, seed wheat, buffalo horns, eggs, and dairy products, and the seemingly constant visits of lonely neighbors, the farm became the center of the community. We were not unduly surprised when our home was designated the post office with Kildahl as its name and Andrew appointed as postmaster. Our post office was officially opened on February 16th, 1885, and continued operating in our name until January 16th, 1893, when it was moved to Maza railroad station, two miles away, and the name of the post office was changed accordingly.

On the whole the post office proved to be a nuisance, more bother and trouble than it was worth. While we were proud to be on the map, even a very small map, when it was moved to Maza it was a relief to the family members still at home. Somebody had to be on hand constantly to serve the occasional patron, but there was little if anything in it financially. To convey some idea of the small volume of post office business transacted, I received a fancy check from Washington in the amount of 18¢ for three month's work. My job requirements were to carry the mail on horseback ten miles between Churchs Ferry and Kildahl three times weekly for a certain percentage of the net earnings of our post office. It was the first check I had ever received and I am sorry I did not keep it, frame it, and display it as a signal recognition

by a beneficent Federal government for services faithfully
rendered. Unused to the ways of the world, I didn't know what
to do with it. I returned it to the Treasurer of the United States
and demanded cash, a medium of exchange which I could
understand. He sent it back with a letter informing me that any
bank or store would exchange it for real money and thereby
contributed to my education in financial matters. Fortunately,
I was relieved of my unremunerative task on July 2nd, 1886,
when a regular stage line was inaugurated between Devils Lake
and Island Lake,[51] with a stop at Kildahl, and which carried
the mail for a much better financial return, I'm sure, than I
received.

About three miles west of Kildahl, beyond Mr. Walker's
holdings, lived a bachelor named Plummer. A somewhat
nondescript, unprepossessing fellow, he usually came for
his mail on Sundays, visited in a desultory fashion, and then
disappeared for another week. The last man on earth any
woman would want, he seemed to me, so I was considerably
surprised and not a little shocked when, one Sunday, he
appeared with a woman whom he introduced as his wife.
Overcoming my momentary astonishment, I congratulated
them and inquired where they had found each other since I
had never seen her before. "Oh," he said, "I just picked her up
on the road." It turned out to be literally true. She, I learned,
had been working for a widow with several children who had
settled near a place called Plunder, and one day in the recent
past had decided to walk to Churchs Ferry. Evidently a fast
hiker, she overtook Mr. Plummer driving with his wagon and
oxen to the same destination. Politely, he offered her a ride
which she accepted. After a bit of conversation he proposed to
her, she accepted him, and when they reached town they were
married. Frankly, after seeing that strong, quite large, capable
looking young woman and hearing her talk, I'm not sure who
picked up whom. At least Plummer had seen, talked to, and had
a chance to size up his bride if only briefly, certainly better than
finding and taking a mail order wife. At any rate, the match
worked out well for Mr. Plummer, at least, because when
she took charge of his farm it flourished. I don't know what

happened to the widow and her children after her hired girl left and got married.

The Sather brother's home, smoke filled, odoriferous, and over-crowded as it was, became a social center for disconsolate bachelor men. The bachelor girls of the community congregated at Kildahl, and made our place their community club, so to speak. Of course, the presence of the post office and the going and coming of customers for our various commodities may have acted as a magnet for the girls, but I think the main attraction was Andrew, a large, energetic, handsome man who wore sideburns and cut quite a dashing figure. Since he never gave any of the bachelor girls a second glance, no encouragement at all, it seems odd that the two bachelor groups never got together; among the two groups no sparks flew, no romances developed. One day towards spring, a group of men were gathered at Al and Nils Sather's when someone remarked that the life they were leading was anything but desirable and expressed the hope that some other, attractive, marriageable females would settle in the community. Another, named Bill, told the group that he had been engaged to a woman in Toronto, but that they had drifted apart and ceased their correspondence. This confession, for some reason, caused considerable hilarity, joshing remarks, and not very discreet questions regarding the lady's appearance, beauty, figure, manners, etc. Jocularly, the suggestion was made that everybody should help Bill compose a letter to the girl proposing marriage, an idea agreed to and immediately implemented. Each man made a suggestion to go into the message, the letter was written and mailed at our post office. It contained, primarily, the proposition that if she had not changed her mind about marrying him, Bill would meet her at a certain hotel in Grand Forks on a designated day and they would be married there and then.

About a week later a letter arrived at Kildahl addressed, to Bill, post marked Toronto, in which she agreed to marry him. With several days grace before his mandatory appearance in Grand Forks, Bill, a heavy drinker, went on a three day spree in Churchs Ferry. On the day before his departure to the arms of his betrothed, half sober, he announced from atop a huge snow drift in downtown Churchs Ferry, that this would be his final binge, that he was going to be married and that no married man had any business getting drunk. As far as I know, Bill was never again intoxicated.

All the letter writers were eager and anxious to see the bride and, after the newly married couple returned, his friends arranged a wedding party. After meeting the girl, some, not very well mannered, I'm afraid, sympathized with Bill because she was not the sweet, beautiful, young thing they had expected from his description of her. Good natured Bill, now content, took no offense, laughed them off, and proved once again that "beauty is in the eye of the beholder." She was, indeed, a good, smart, capable woman and she and Bill, deeply in love, lived happily together.

When information circulated in the community that a young couple with a baby had settled northwest of us, it was heralded as an event of no small significance. The grapevine of communication carried a rising tide of excitement and it was soon evident to all that something had to be done to mark the occasion. Word went out that on a specified Sunday afternoon, all interested settlers were to meet at the home of the young family. When the day came almost everybody who lived within a ten mile radius, and a few from farther away, was in attendance to see, hold, fondle, and drool over the wondrous boy child. If ever a young mother had occasion to be proud of her offspring, that one did, with compliments as to the baby's size, appearance, and goodness heaped upon her. A purse was raised for the infant there and then, and every one of the bachelor men had to pay a high price, as much as $5.00, which they willingly did, for the privilege of holding the baby for a short time. I don't know what became of that child who started life in such a celebrated fashion. If only half of the good wishes showered upon him were realized, he should have risen high in his subsequent career and life.

27

AMBITION REKINDLED, DREAMS FULFILLED

It seemed like a surprise party when Rev. Aaberg, whom we had met and for whom I had worked in Grand Forks in 1880, drove up to the house and proceeded to make himself at home with us. When the congregation he had started in Grand Forks was flourishing and could do without him, he moved to Devils Lake and made it the center of his ministry where in three years he would found Aaberg Academy.[52] He was out in the field, he told us, with a view of gathering people for worship and, when conditions were right, to organize congregations.

While we were delighted to see him and he us, which created an atmosphere much like a family reunion, he was keenly disappointed to find us the only settlers with a Norwegian background in that part of the country. He could not understand why we had settled amongst people neither Norwegian nor Lutheran and we had some difficulty making him understand that he had it backwards; that we were the first to arrive and others had settled around us, a development over which we had no control. Even after the light dawned, he, with magnificent hindsight, declared it a pity and a mistake for if we had settled in a Norwegian-dominated community, we would have been in position to be a strong influence in organizing and maintaining a congregation. Unable to argue with the perverseness of his position, we fell silent, transfixed by his sheer wrongheadedness. Despite his inability to get that matter straight in his mind, he was a warm, humble, and friendly man whom we welcomed as a pastor to us. He returned to our home as often as he could and conducted worship services including the sacrament of communion which was appreciated by all the family members.

We didn't realize at first that the arrival of Rev. Aaberg in our midst was a harbinger of things to come, first, for the entire family, and second, for my future, but his influence was soon felt. He sought to establish congregations as close to the frontier on the northern plains as possible, and was indefatigable in that work. Not finding fallow ground for a church group in our immediate neighborhood, he nevertheless continued his search for Lutherans and rounded up enough of us in and around Churchs Ferry to begin regular services in a rented building in the town. The group organized in 1885 as Antiochia Congregation and our family was part of it, which not only brought great comfort to us all but regularized our lives and extended our social horizons to others of our faith and nationality. In 1895, seven years after I left the farm to attend school in Northfield, Minnesota, a split occurred in the congregation. The dissidents joined another group and erected a church in Churchs Ferry, while the original congregation moved approximately three miles southwest by south of town and built Antiochia Church.[53] After the split my parents remained faithful to the latter group, traveled about thirteen miles to attend services, and finally were buried in Antiochia churchyard.

Rev. Aaberg's presence and influence revived my old ambition to be a clergyman, a goal I had lost sight of in my desire to secure and develop as much land as possible. I had caught a severe case of land fever, a contagious disease, and had fallen in love with the wild, seemingly limitless expanse of prairie which I found constantly fascinating. To become a farmer on a large scale was not a too far-fetched dream and would be a satisfying way of life. I had even selected a location for my future home, and in my imagination had populated it with a wife and children and equipped the farm with the finest implements money could buy. In the presence of Rev. Aaberg, that dream faded and the old desire to be a pastor returned with such force I never again deviated from its spell. I experienced a true calling to the ministry and would do everything possible to fulfill the requirements for that vocation.

My young brother, Nils, was absent from Kildahl during the 1885-86 academic year attending school at Redwing Seminary, an academy in Redwing, Minnesota. That was during the period our older brother, Nathan, was acting president of the academy. When he returned in the early summer of '86, it was obvious he was unhappy with school. Soon to turn only 15, he was restless and discontented with his life and surroundings. He spent quite a good deal of time in Churchs Ferry or Devils Lake, evidently making new friends, and to escape farming, which he hated.

In the fall of that year, while our parents were in Goodhue County, to see Nathan and old friends, Nils simply didn't come back from a visit with some cowboys he had become acquainted with during the previous weeks. Given Nils's fascination with the west, horses, and cowboys, his departure was inevitable, but it caused my parents and the rest of us a good deal of concern. In time, he wrote from Miles City, Montana, where he found work with some large cattle and horse outfits as a wrangler and cowboy, skills he learned very quickly. He worked for some years with The American Cattle Company and became expert in his work, and during his life as a cowboy he originated the first "rope corral," fashioned from discarded Sharps rifle barrels and lariats, an "invention" used in the west ever since.[54]

In 1895 Nils settled on a ranch located along the south bank of the Yellowstone River in the Horton area, just west of Miles City. On his large spread he grazed many cattle at first and when the beef market failed after the World War[55] he turned to raising sheep for the wool market. In 1896 Nils married Miss Anna Johnson and they have raised two children. At the time I write these words, he owns some eighteen sections of grazing land and seems to be doing well with sheep but recently he has been planting sugar beets in his extensive bottomlands along the river. After many years he has returned to farming, an occupation he despised and deserted when he was a boy.[56]

In 1887 we were still living in the original sodded house and, even with the departure of Nils, we needed more room. We also needed a new barn to shelter our growing herd of cattle, our oxen, and our horses, and store their fodder and straw. We also needed additional outbuildings and, when I left to go back to school, which would have to be soon if at all, only Andrew and Matilda would remain near our parents, and the burden of building the new structures would fall on them, which didn't seem fair treatment. Josie had been going to school when she could and had begun teaching others when she was only 14 while we lived in Marshall County, Minnesota. She had left home in the fall of 1886 to seek more schooling in Grand Forks and could not be counted upon for help around the farm.

Beginning in the autumn of 1887, Andrew and I planned our new buildings and intended to start construction in early spring, 1888. We would have to hire others to help us finish everything by fall of the latter year. When spring came we began construction of the new house, which we sited near the badger hole well we had dug a few years earlier and that continued to furnish abundant, cool, clear water. The house had a basement including a root cellar, six rooms on the main floor and four upstairs, and faced south. The old sod stable was replaced with a large barn about 150 feet east of the house. We planted trees north and west of the buildings and cultivated them like a corn field. We planted a few rows of willows north and west of the other trees to serve as a windbreak. The willows were put in as a precautionary measure to protect the other trees from storms which were generally nor'westers. The willows grew very fast and did their job admirably. We also built common farm structures such as a granary, machine shed, poultry house, hog pen, etc.

Matilda married and moved out but remained in the neighborhood with her husband, Carl F. Solberg. Later on, when Andrew married Andrea Skogsmark in 1892, a separate house for our parents was built in the most sheltered part of the home plat. Later a windmill was added and a shed to house the well was built as an addition to the barn to allow the stock to be watered without exposing them to winter storms. The land sloped in every direction from the well and new house. After his marriage, Andrew farmed his own land, our parents', and mine, which I rented to him. When the land I owned had paid for my education, I sold it to him, and he became what I at one time had planned for myself, a farmer on a large scale. He was popular, handsome, articulate, and successful.

Unfortunately, he died in 1908, age 54. Matilda, perhaps the best of all of us, followed him in 1910, age 58. Life was precarious in those days—any number of diseases could and did kill people suddenly, with little or no warning. Before my parents died, they saw four of their nine children die prematurely, a distressing and unnatural, though not uncommon, occurrence in many families of that era. But I have gotten ahead of my story.

Until the time Andrew was married, we had all concentrated our efforts on developing Father's farm. All the buildings were placed there and his land was the first to be cultivated. We had everything in common and did not think very much about individual interests, but when Andrew brought his bride home it dawned on us that there would have to be a change in policy. We began to think of each other's land as individual entities and to think in terms of "mine" and not "ours." Since 1886, when I turned 21, I had acquired a total of 400 acres, 240 of which was excellent soil and the remaining 160 acres, a tree claim, not so good. In 1888, prior to going off to school, I put the 240 acres under cultivation and a portion of the tree claim, and rented all of it to Andrew who farmed it together with his own land. I not only received rent for it but shared in profits from the crops harvested in the fall. In that way I was able to finance my education. It all seemed like a Godsend to me. I would fulfill my ambition to become a minister while at the same time my parents would be protected and cared for by Andrew. Everyone was happy with the arrangement—a perfect agreement.

In late fall of 1888, with new construction nearly completed, crops near harvesting, and agreements made, Josie and I left home to go to school. She, as I mentioned earlier, had been going on and off to school during the past two years, but she wanted more. She had been teaching, too, but wanted to earn a true teacher's certificate. She had saved some money and we were happy to go together. But first, we had to say goodbye. I, at least, found that bidding my parents and Andrew farewell was somewhat more difficult than I had anticipated. It was one of the few times that I have wept since I grew into manhood. It was not only that I was leaving them, but I felt it was the parting of our ways and that the congenial relationship which we had enjoyed was at an end. Of course, I would visit them as often as I could but it wouldn't be the same. We had gone through many hardships together, had been a comfort and solace to each other, and had encouraged and cheered each other with our hopes for the future. We had seen the realization of those hopes, to some extent, and yet different from what we had expected. After we parted, I would take a road that would lead me in a different direction. There is an old Scandinavian proverb which translated means: "The threshold step is the hardest step." I found it to be true.

IV

MINNESOTA AGAIN

*Harold B. Kildahl,
ordination portrait, 1898..*

Carrie E. Olson, 1898..

28

BACK TO SCHOOL

My brother Nathan was then pastor of Vangs[57] and Urland congregations which were about twenty miles east of Northfield. The second dugout in which we had lived in Goodhue County was only a quarter of a mile from Urland Church, so Josie and I were getting back to familiar territory. We left home early to enable us to spend a few days visiting at Nathan's parsonage, which was a large and, in my eyes, a beautiful home across the road from the Vangs Church.

It seemed like a revelation to go to worship services there the Sunday after our arrival. The visit made such an impression on me that I can see and hear it yet; Nathan's presence and sermon were powerful. I had never before seen or heard anything like it. Nathan is considered by many today [in the 1920s and 30s] to be the greatest preacher that the Norwegians have produced in America and I believe he was, and not just because he was my brother. I heard him preach many times since 1888 but he never made such an impression on me as he did the first time I heard him in that rural church. I began to hope that I might become such a pastor as he.

Nathan took us to Northfield to St. Olaf School where the winter term was to begin the next day. Eight years or so had passed since the family moved away from Northfield and Josie and I noticed that many changes had occurred in the town we knew so well from our childhood. Our brother re-introduced us to Professor Mohn, who was President of the school. He did not appear to have changed whatsoever over the years and although we had changed a great deal he seemed to recognize us. He was happy to see us and asked many questions about our parents. We were also introduced to Professor Ytterboe,[58] who was Dean of Men. He was a commanding figure of a man with a kind smile who won my immediate respect and admiration.

He invited Josie, Nathan, and me to supper at his home. We had registered from Kildahl, Dakota Territory, and at the supper table he asked me how large Kildahl was, and innocently, I told him I thought he weighed about 180 pounds, which provoked laughter from the ladies, the Dean, and Nathan. I had never thought of Kildahl as a town, which, of course, it wasn't—merely a post office.

That evening there was an entertainment in the chapel and I happened to be seated next to a man who introduced himself to me. He said, "I understand your name is Kildahl. My name is Gross." There had been a student at St. Olaf School "by that name who boarded with us in 1876. I was surprised to find him still there twelve years later. Jokingly, I said, "Well, for land's sake, haven't you finished school yet?" He laughed infectiously, in which I joined, and finally said, "Yes, I have. I am one of the professors here." After the fun subsided I decided I had better curb my tongue a bit—keep my mouth shut. I had spoken impulsively twice that evening and if I did not keep still I might get into real trouble. As things turned out, my coming to St. Olaf was memorable to both Dean Ytterboe and Professor Gross; neither forgot that first day of mine. Both have alluded to our first meetings accompanied by merriment and laughter. I never knew whether they were laughing with me or at me, but all turned out well.

The next day my life at St. Olaf took on a more serious aspect. Professor Ytterboe examined me in order, as he said, to find out what class I would fit into. He started with arithmetic, which was always punishment for me. He asked if I knew algebra. I told him that I did not know what she looked like. "Have you had percentages?" I had to reveal some more ignorance. "How about fractions?" Nothing. I thought all those terms must come from higher education, so I told him that he did not seem to have my number. With some exasperation he asked me just what did I know about arithmetic? I told him, "I can add, subtract, multiply, and divide if I am given plenty of time." He asked if I knew long division. I told him I had heard about it but I had never seen it. He looked at me as though he was examining a specimen in a museum, so I told him that I had best make a clean breast of it. I confessed that

I had attended a public school for two years before we moved out west and that it was ten years since I had been in a school room. I added that I was afraid St. Olaf did not have any class elementary enough for me and that I had better begin in some primary school.

The expression on the Dean's face changed from curiosity to sympathy. He asked if I had studied grammar, which I answered in the negative. He selected a book and asked me to choose any page and read aloud. As I complied he grew more cheerful: when I finished reading a couple of paragraphs, he asked if I knew any history. With that question my face must have brightened because he started smiling. I told him that I had read United States history and world history by myself but in Norwegian. His smile broadened and he told me that St. Olaf offered a class that he thought I would fit into but he wished I had come at the beginning of the fall term as it would have been easier for me. I assured him I was familiar with hard work and felt confident I could catch up on the material I had missed. He informed me that a number of older students, like me, whose education had been neglected, had enrolled that year and that the school had arranged what he called a sub-preparatory class for them which I could join. He assured me that the teachers did a great deal of personal work with the students in that special class.

The group of students given that special attention were mostly men and women between 20 and 30 years of age who, like myself, for one reason or another, had not been in a position to attend school during that time of life when most children do. We certainly needed all the help, understanding, and attention the instructional staff could give us, collectively and individually. When I review it, years later, I have utmost admiration and gratitude for their patience and kindness. I never before realized the resourcefulness, effort, and skill required to jar loose a stagnant mind and make it function. Fractions were like a Chinese puzzle to us and English grammar seemed an impenetrable thicket. The class became a mutual sympathizing society and it is more than probable that some of my classmates might have given up in despair if it were not for the encouragement we received from each other and from our teachers. That first term was certainly anything but a happy existence. Searching the dictionary in order to determine the placement of a word as a part of speech, as I remember, was a painstaking, excruciating process. There was one member of the class, a man named Sabin, who became a favorite of all the rest of us because he could tell us what part of speech a word was without the aid of a dictionary.

I managed to pass the examination at the end of the winter term, but I felt dissatisfied with the result of my test in fractions. I asked for permission to take it over the next term, which was granted after discussion by the instructional staff in a faculty meeting. I would like to have obtained a copy of the minutes of that meeting.

29

GLIMPSES OF STUDENT LIFE

In those days St. Olaf School consisted of the Old Main and a large frame building which was used as a dormitory for the girls. We boys and young men lived on the third floor of the Old Main. Our rooms were heated by stoves in each room and we had to carry firewood up to our rooms. It was no small job to carry loads of wood about a block to the building and then up two long flights of stairs to our quarters. Some wag pointed out that all that work was really a blessing because the wood warmed us twice—first in the exertion of carrying it and then by burning it. He wasn't pummeled too badly.

There were no bathing facilities on campus when I came to St. Olaf late in 1888. In order to keep clean we had to take sponge baths. It was quite an event when we returned to school one fall (1890, I think) and found a bathroom in the basement. A group of us were in the bathing room expressing satisfaction and appreciation of it when someone conveyed the information that we would be expected to pay ten cents every time we took a bath. It seemed a prohibitive price to some of us, and the spirit of the group was on the verge of changing from appreciation to indignation, when Professor Mohn appeared among us, no doubt attracted by the loud argumentation. His mere presence tended to calm things down but he was helped by the arrival of another student bearing an old fashioned wooden wash tub. It almost dropped out of his hands when he saw the school's President, who asked him what he was going to do with the tub. The student, who had a strong Norwegian accent and great difficulty with English, blurted "I vant to bat." "Well then," said Professor Mohn, "you better go out to the baseball field," and he laughed in his good natured way. That touch of humor, which we all enjoyed, put an end to our altercation about the cost of cleanliness. But the real joke of the episode was that it was the only time that the boy with the tub was ever known to be interested in taking a bath.

By the time I enrolled in St. Olaf School, a college and seminary of sorts was being established there by a group calling itself a Brotherhood. They had formed themselves in 1885 because of a predestination squabble. [Now largely forgotten.] The Brotherhood's theological students taking seminary courses conducted a weekly prayer meeting which interested me and I attended regularly, at first. I marveled at the length and fervency of their prayers and felt sinful when I compared myself to them and felt quite unworthy to be in their company. At one of the meetings I sat, unfortunately, near a student whose prayers were powerful and earnest but he had such an offensive breath I had to move away from him. It seemed to me that even an admirable prayer associated with such halitosis could not be acceptable to God. That experience lowered considerably the esteem in which I had held those theologians, and their prayer meetings did not attract me as much thereafter.

The kitchen and dining room were located in the basement of Old Main. There were five long tables extending across the room. The boys and men occupied three of the tables and the girls the other two. The tables were covered with white oil cloth which hung down over the sides and ends. New students were sometimes "initiated" to our midst by the ingenious transformation of the overhanging oil cloth into a trough. The trough conveyed, say, a cup of water to the lap of the unsuspecting stranger, guided to the exact spot by the conspirator sitting next to him. The victim was usually a newcomer, away from home for the first time, shy, and dressed in his best clothes. The water treatment did nothing for his self esteem. If he was bashful to begin with, he was now embarrassed to the point of remaining seated until few if any students remained to witness his humiliating exit from the room. Of course I, older and wiser than many of my fellow students, never participated in those childish pranks!

The bread served in the commons was cheap and plain, which was to be expected, but occasionally it was hardly edible. There were times when the bread was so doughy that the boys molded it into statuary. The butter, too, often left something to be desired as far as taste went, caused by trying to make it last longer, but butter is a commodity that does not improve with age. Delegations of students were sent to Dean Ytterboe to protest about the bad food. After the second group visited him, the Dean came to the dining room, sat with us, and ate the same food we were served. In order to impress him with the age of the butter when it was especially rancid, somebody, just before meal time, had thrown or placed a rather large chunk of it onto a beam just over Dean Ytterboe's chair. During the meal the butter melted and began to drip down on him. A rigid examination was conducted, but the culprit was never discovered. Whoever he was, we all owed him a debt of gratitude because the quality of the butter immediately improved, as did the consistency of the bread.

One Thanksgiving Day we were served turkey and all the trimmings. I learned later that the birds were donated by Mrs. George Olson, who later became my mother-in-law. There was plenty of food for everyone but late in the evening a desire for more turkey overcame a group of boys rooming on the third floor. Two were chosen (or volunteered) to try to gain entrance to the pantry and "borrow" one of the leftover fowls, if, indeed, the rumor that a few had not been consumed during the meal was true. It was. The raid was successful and a turkey feast was held in one of the rooms behind locked doors. The next morning the bird was missed and a search instigated but the mystery seemed unfathomable until a sharp-eyed investigator spotted a boy whose vest was greasy on the outside and his coat in the same condition on the inside. The lamentable (not to say disgusting) condition of his clothes proved to be such strong circumstantial evidence that a confession followed and the mystery was solved.

Gradually the number of girls enrolled in school increased to such an extent that two dining tables were not sufficient for them. Some of the boys were boarding elsewhere which created space for the additional girls at the middle table, but the school authorities were hesitant about mixing the sexes. I had noticed that Dean Ytterboe had a worried expression on his face and it made me a little uneasy when he called me aside and told me about his predicament. He asked me if I was willing to change my place. He knew I had such high regard for St. Olaf School that I would do anything for it, even sit next to a girl! I consented and it was with considerable pride that I took my new seat in the dining room. To be trusted with such a responsibility was enough to make any young man chesty. I did not feel so proud, however, when the young lady similarly trusted took her place next to me, a girl whom I particularly disliked. I tried to overcome my feelings regarding her and I hope she never discovered them. At any rate, by changing tables and mingling the sexes, we were instrumental in enhancing true coeducation at St. Olaf, although I've always wished I could have had a choice in selecting my meal partner. The date of that event should have been recorded as a milestone in the history of the school for it not only began the dismantling of the policy of rigid separation of the sexes which had been the norm since 1874 but resulted in many courtships and marriages of future St. Olaf couples.

For a short while we had a matron supervising our housekeeping and deportment who was officious and hateful and I am reasonably sure had no friends among the students. She owned a little dog which she fondled and spoiled endlessly. The constant pampering of the animal aroused antagonism toward him by the students who found ways to cause the dog and its mistress, if not pain, certainly distress and unpleasantness. I've always felt a little sorry for the mutt, an innocent victim of unfortunate associations, but I've never known any other dog that had so much attention showered upon him. His owner tried to protect her pet from all the "solicitude" shown him by the students but the more she tried to do so the worse it became for him. Her safeguards and precautions simply challenged the ingenuity of the students, and they outdid themselves.

Resentment of the matron reached a climax on a 6th of November. I don't claim the events of that memorable date were the result of a conspiracy but there is no doubt concerted action was undertaken by some students. The out-of-favor matron came down to supper attired in a white dress. Somebody had dipped the dog's feet in ink and when he jumped into her lap, the effect on the dress was disastrous. The lady, enraged, arose to leave the table but was unable to do so in a decisive manner because the chair she was occupying arose with her, affixed firmly to the back of her lap by a generous supply of sticky syrup that had somehow been spilled on its seat. In high dudgeon the lady, in a now besmirched white frock, extricated herself from her tenacious trap amid a profound, almost shocking silence. Shooting looks of hatred and haughty disdain from her flashing eyes, the grim lipped figure escaped the room with few vestiges of remaining dignity. After her exit, a few titters triggered explosive, uncontrollable, yes, triumphant laughter, and even a few cheers. It was a hilarious salute to the college's birthday.

The result of that unforgettable scene was a new matron, who did much to improve the spirit and morale of the students. The uproar in the dining room that resulted in the first matron's resignation was thoroughly investigated by the school's authorities but the perpetrator or perpetrators of the "tragedy" were never discovered. The final effort to identify the culprit or culprits ended when President Mohn called the students together in the chapel and lectured us about high ideals, nobility of character, and the courage of confession. He then left us to ourselves to contemplate our sins and to fathom the mystery if we could. We did not succeed in accomplishing the latter, but we did adopt a two-part resolution: first, that dogs can and do wander into ink pots occasionally, and, second, syrup pitchers can and do accidentally tip over. No more was ever said of the incident or of the abrupt departure from campus of that overbearing, insufferable matron.

The first year I attended St. Olaf I was there only during the winter term. In the 1889-90 school year I attended the winter and spring terms. During the next two years I took not only the full course load each term but a few additional hours of study so that when I finished the academy requirements I had also completed half of the studies needed for the freshman class of the college, which by 1892 had become an official institution of the United Norwegian Lutherans and was no longer controlled or dominated by the Brotherhood.

The class that was graduated from the Academy in 1892 consisted of 27 members, including three young ladies. We were a motley aggregation. There were men with full beards and some with mustaches; one was married; one had side whiskers and wore a Prince Albert suit, simulating a clergyman, which he became later on with no preparatory study of Theology. There was a shortage of pastors at that time and several of the graduates, including him, responded to the call with what was equal only to a high school education, but they were elderly men with considerable life experience. Some of those men have done remarkably well despite their scanty training and preparation.

It fell to my lot to write the class history. As I have mentioned, the class included three girls. I remember little of that history other than that I alluded to our class as a strawberry shortcake with only three sweet strawberries in it. I was quite a flatterer. The graduation ceremonies were to take place June 12th, 1892. A few days before the great event I received word that my brother Andrew was to be married to Andrea Skogsmark on June 10th at Rock Dell, Minnesota. I arranged to have somebody else read my immortal words in the event I could not get back in time from the wedding, but I returned on the morning of the 12th and read the history myself.

Graduation from St. Olaf Academy was considered to be quite an important event. It meant as much or more to be graduated from a high school or academy then than it is to be graduated from a college now. [In the 1920s and early 30s.] I believe I was the only member of that class who went on, finished the college course, and obtained a baccalaureate degree.

30

MY COLLEGE YEARS

In the fall of 1892 I enrolled as a freshman in St. Olaf College, but as I had done some of the first year work while still in the Academy, I added a course or two of sophomore level classes. During my entire college career I was divided between two such brackets, always registering for advanced courses ahead of my nominal class which enabled me to be graduated in three years instead of the usual four. That procedure saddled me with a heavy load all through college, but it meant saving a precious year which I deemed important because I would be 30 years old when I finished in 1895. There was a great need for preachers in the burgeoning church and I meant to be one of them as soon as possible.

Two occurrences are memorable to me from my undergraduate years. The first was some sound advice I have never forgotten. At the conclusion of our sophomore year, (1893) a number of the older students left college and entered the theological seminary. As I was one of the oldest I felt a strong urge to do likewise but decided to consult President Mohn before making such a precipitate move. When we met, he listened to me patiently and I thought I was persuading him to accept my plan. When I rested my case he smiled and said, "Well, Kildahl, I appreciate all you have said but I don't think it would be a wise move. Of course, if you want to be a sawhorse all your life, you better enter the seminary now." I was very much taken aback and asked him to explain what he meant. He smiled and said, "You see, there are men in the ministry and there are sawhorses. The men will move the sawhorses about just as a carpenter moves his when he wants to use them. That's the way it will be in the ministry. Are you sure you want to be a sawhorse?" I saw his point, thanked him for his time and advice, and assured him I had no ambition to be a sawhorse; I would remain in college and earn my degree. I have been thankful to President Mohn ever since for his candor and directness. If he had taken an hour to explain the importance of a college education, he could not have done so more clearly or emphatically.

The second outstanding event that has had a lasting effect on me occurred during the beginning of the fall term in 1894 when I met Carrie Emilie Olson. She and her sister, Ella, from Taylor, Wisconsin, entered St. Olaf College as first year students that fall. Both were outstanding girls in appearance, dress, manners, and accomplishments. Carrie was a fine solo singer with a rich and powerful soprano voice who made a great hit with me by singing "Ben Bolt," a popular song of the time. I admired her, though, only at a distance. Both Carrie and Ella became the objects of competition by a number of the boys but the sisters reacted coolly and had no, or at least did not indicate that they had any, favorites. I feared, though, that a classmate of mine was making headway and would win in the contest for Carrie, but to his consternation and my delight, she accepted an invitation to be my guest at the Commencement dinner in the spring of 1895, when I completed my college work.

I have gotten a little ahead of myself in my eagerness to write about Carrie Olson. I must go back to my last summer vacation, just before I met her, which I spent partly in the service of an organization headed by Rev. Carl Raughland of Minneapolis. The purpose of the group was to encourage the establishment of Young People's Societies in congregations throughout the Twin City area and as far afield as possible. My intent to become a minister remained firm and in as much as the future of any organization lies in it's youth, it struck me as a sensible and far-sighted organization and activity. I was engaged to travel and promote the cause in as many churches as I could reach, and was a valuable experience for me. I assumed all pastors would be favorably disposed to our cause but I found some who were against the whole concept. They held the belief that young people had been baptized and

confirmed in the church and did not need a separate society.
Some were indifferent. Some consented to let me speak in
their churches but, instead of wishing me well or showing any
enthusiasm for my work, they seemed to consider me with
a degree of suspicion. Some of the pastors, however, were
welcoming, kind, and cooperative and encouraged me in the
young people's cause. Rev. Raughland possessed foresight, was
an inspirational leader, and was vitally interested in the young
people of the United Lutheran Church. When we consider the
extensive young people's movement active today and their
extensive travel, even across the continent, to attend their large
biennial conventions [in the late 20s and early 30s] we know
we have made tremendous progress since it all started in 1894.
We also know that Rev. Raughland's enthusiasm for his work
and vision of the future youth movement was not misplaced.

Commencement is always a gala event at all colleges
and universities, including St. Olaf. The classes were small in
those days and the students to be graduated were looked upon
with envy and admiration by the rest of the student body. Plans
for the great day were made long in advance and relatives and
friends of all students, not only of the graduating class, came
long distances to partake in the festivities and enjoy the day.
Under the colors of Old Glory, raised to the top of Old Main,
class and society meetings were held and social groups met. It
was something like a family reunion.

We were a class of only six men (but which was
considered to be quite large.) We were C. M. Weswig, Ole
Glesne, J. A. E. Naess, Albert Haugen, Sever Svien, and
myself. We were close friends then and that comradeship has
continued ever since, and has proved a priceless benefit of our
college education through the years. I appreciate my classmates
without any reservation and I am proud of being a member of
the St. Olaf class of 1895. The custom of the time required each
candidate for graduation to deliver an oration, which we did.
The subject for my oration was "Why Are We Thus?" I have
only a dim memory of it and I wish I had saved the manuscript;
I would like to review my solution to that momentous question.

With College authorities presiding and with faculty, friends, and relatives present to witness the ceremonies, the six of us received our hard-earned and long sought degrees.

It seemed like leaving home all over again when I left the college after graduation. Students and teachers were like members of a large family that was breaking up. But in truth the college still retained a hold on me because President Mohn engaged me to work as a field man for the school during the summer of 1895. I entered into that work of finding students and raising funds with the desire to do all I could so as to repay St. Olaf for what it had done for me. I continued that activity until August when I had to call a halt and go home to North Dakota to help with bringing in the harvest.

My years in Northfield attending the academy and the college had been difficult in some ways but also rewarding; I had found a girl who would become my wife a few years ahead, had forged friendship with a group of men that would last a lifetime, had been guided by wise men whom I admired and respected, and, equally important, I had finally and fully found myself, knew where I was going, and what I would do with the rest of my life. The rewards heavily outweighed any hardship or difficulty I had encountered on the way.

31

SEMINARY, ENGAGEMENT, AND CALL

My route to Minneapolis and the seminary went by way of Maza, North Dakota to help my brother and folks, as I have mentioned, harvest the bountiful crops of that year. I had a stake in that crop since it provided me with the necessary funds for the continuation of my education at the seminary. I had been 23 years old before starting back to school in 1888, but I believe the time I had spent in acquiring and cultivating the land was well worth it. The income derived from the farm relieved me of any financial embarrassment while I was obtaining my education.

During the brief time I was at home I had several heart to heart talks with my parents about spiritual concerns which were a great help to me. They actuated a deeper examination of my faith, my supposed insufficiency for my vocation, and a deeper search for God's sustaining grace. That interlude at home with my parents was of special significance to me because I had the opportunity to become better acquainted with my father. A man of few words, his life as a semi-invalid at best had perhaps enhanced a potential inferiority complex, but he was a fine grained man with a naturally kind disposition. He made it a rule to keep still if he could not say anything good about a person. He was a graduate of a normal as well as a business school in Norway, but he was also a knowledgeable theologian and very well read. His advice to me as I was about to enter the seminary consisted of three parts: one, to think before I spoke; two, avoid the outwardly pious; and three, always put others' needs before my own. He said he had tried to live by those precepts, and although he hadn't always succeeded, they, combined with unwavering faith in God's word, had enabled him to live a deep and happy Christian life. When I bade my parents farewell, I knew that short sojourn at home had been well and truly spent.

My trip to Minneapolis was still on a detour, this time back to Northfield, but only for three days to visit friends who seemed glad to see me. The days slipped by and before I knew it I was in the metropolis preparing to embark on the final phase of my educational journey to the ministry. In 1892 and 93 a group of dissidents had broken away from the United Norwegian Lutheran Church and formed the Free Church, taking Augsburg College and, theretofore the principal Lutheran Seminary, with them. The United Lutherans adapted themselves to the emergency situation the schism caused by renting the large Zacharius Building located on Franklin Avenue and 26th in south Minneapolis, and establishing not only a seminary, but an academy and college as well. All in all it was an impressive institution.

It was with, not exactly fear and trembling, but, certainly a few qualms that, on September 26th, 1895, I presented myself to the president of the new seminary, Dr. M. O. Bockman. Accompanying my slight trepidation was a feeling of joy that circumstances and hard work had made it possible for me to realize my long-cherished ambition to enter the ministry. I had met Dr. Bockman before but only casually at church meetings; we were not total strangers to each other which helped put me at my ease. My credentials were satisfactory, he told me, and everything was in order to permit me to enroll. A list of books was given me and after a few words of welcome and encouragement, the meeting with Dr. Bockman was completed. I was now, or soon would be, a seminarian, joining four other St. Olaf alumni who entered with me that fall. Three of them were my classmates; Naess, Svien, and Glesne. The fourth was E. B. Wallom of the class of 1894. Naturally the five of us spent a great deal of our spare time together.

The seminary was formally opened on October 9th with appropriate ceremony and the next day our classwork began, which was altogether different from anything we had experienced at St. Olaf. It consisted largely of lectures and note taking. Occasionally a question was asked of a student and sometimes a student posed a question. The faculty consisted of President Bockman, Dr. F. A. Schmidt, and Dr. E. G. Lund. Almost immediately I was drafted by Rev. Gerhard Rasmussen, pastor of Bethlehem Church, to assist him in various duties. I was also elected president of his Young Peoples' Society. By the end of the second week of school I found myself fully occupied. I welcomed the additional duties because they contributed to my training.

The students conducted a boarding club in the basement of the building. As most of them were short of funds, the great attraction of the club was its low costs. I believe a student could eat for less than $1.50 per week. I liked neither the quality of the food nor the manner of the service, and I was not the only one who felt that way. The up-shot was that twelve of us organized a private boarding club located a block from the seminary. We were fortunate in securing an excellent cook and housekeeper to prepare our food for us and keep the quarters clean and neat. Each member paid her 50¢ a week and, in alphabetical order, each served a week as landlord. During his term of office, the landlord paid all bills and kept all receipts. When all twelve had served their terms, the twelve sets of receipts were added up and averaged out. If one landlord's expenditures were below the average he paid the difference and if another's was over he was refunded from the kitty. The system was obviously fair, worked well, and everyone involved was happy with the plan. The general contentment of our group generated jealousy among some members of the school basement boarding club, who could not refrain from making snide remarks such as "How are things going over in paradise?" That particular barb was not very clever because the obvious rejoinder was to inquire how conditions were in the other place.

One day Rev. A. J. Haupt, A Lutheran pastor in St. Paul, visited the seminary and Dr. Bockman looking for a student who could preach in the English language and would help him foster a mission he had started in North St. Paul. I realized it was a chance to obtain some real experience in preparing and delivering sermons. I responded to his appeal, was accepted, and then pleasantly surprised when he told me he could not pay more than $25.00 per month, because I had not expected more than streetcar fare. He desired my services every Sunday, which was a drawback because I wanted to hear other preachers. I arranged with one of my chums, Glesne, to take over every other Sunday and earn half the fee, a plan that was satisfactory to Rev. Haupt. We continued that schedule during the first two years of our seminary training, although during the first summer vacation I carried on the work alone. At the conclusion of the second school year, Rev. Haupt secured a young pastor for the mission and Glesne and I were released. Both of us appreciated that work experience and our association with Rev. Haupt, who was a capable, devoted pastor. And both of us had liked the extra income, too.

My final summer vacation (1897) was spent assisting Rev. J. M. O. Ness in and around Perley, Minnesota. His charge consisted of four large churches, three on the Minnesota side of the Red River and one in North Dakota, all served exclusively in the Norwegian language. I had had considerable experience preaching in English in North St. Paul, and that summer, as assistant to Rev. Ness, I acquired similar experience in Norwegian, which would prepare me for a call in either or both languages. There was a great deal to do in that parish, as the reader can well imagine, with four large, separate congregations to which to minister including confirmation instruction, mid-week meetings, pastoral calls on the ill, aged, and infirm, as well as other work.

Four big churches required a great deal of preaching, too, and that meant I spent much time in sermon preparation, often working with the pastor, who helped me patiently and unstintingly. We often studied sermon construction and sermon outlines together, which made him a kind of tutor to me. He was a brilliant man, a thorough student, and an effective and versatile teacher, but, unfortunately, he was too language-minded, too erudite, for his congregations. He talked over their heads and did not really communicate with them. But, on the whole, I consider that summer's experience as a Godsend because it gave me an insight into rural church activity that helped me later in my own work, and I became acquainted with people who are still my friends.

Two memories of Perley, unconnected with the churches, remain with me. Both, however, are related to the unusually wet summer in that area, with too much rain for the good of the crops. Evidently the farmers had experienced similar deluges before because some large drainage ditches had been dug, yet part of the land was submerged. For the fun of it, I built a dam in one of those ditches and photographed the resulting waterfall. It was a delightful surprise to the residents when I showed them the picture of a waterfall taken in their own community, where there was hardly a hill in sight. Some boasted of their very own Minnehaha Falls!

While that memory is pleasant and joyful, the other is less so. It is of the prevalence of mosquitoes that created a pesky, prolonged problem that summer. People carried large iron kettles in their wagons for making heavy smudges and men wore mosquito netting over their hats while working in the fields. Without those precautions work was impossible and driving a team with the wind was punishment indeed. I had had considerable experience with the insects during my pioneer days in Dakota Territory but nothing I suffered then matched the torture inflicted by the Perley brand of mosquitoes. They truly were in a class by themselves—without doubt a superior breed of the creatures.

The seminary faculty asked me to spend my last Christmas vacation in Larimore, North Dakota, where there was a temporary pastoral vacancy. I complied, caught a train, and arrived in time to deliver the sermon on Christmas Day, speak at a Christmas Tree program, and schedule a number of services both in and near the town, but I became ill and had to take to a bed for two days. The doctor who was called in to look after me advised me to be quiet and inactive for a week and not exert myself. Since Larimore is less than a hundred miles from Maza, I decided to go home for the remainder of the vacation period. Although I was happy to spend a brief time with my family, I was sorry to have lost the opportunity of ministering to the people of Larimore.

When I returned to Minneapolis I found two letters awaiting me. When I opened them I was thrilled to find they contained letters of call from congregations. One was from a rural community in northwestern Minnesota who wanted a pastor to work exclusively in Norwegian, and the other was from a city congregation requiring only English from me. I would have preferred to accept the latter call, but when I entered the seminary I promised the Lord that if He would use me in His service I would accept the first call He sent me. The call to the rural community bore the earlier date and postmark which left me no choice in the matter. I did not ask any questions, did not look over the field, but considered it as the prior call from the Lord. I spoke to Dr. Bockman about it, told him of my vow to God, and he agreed that the matter was settled for me. Accordingly, on February 19th, 1898, I sent my acceptance to the call committee representing the congregations of the parish. The call consisted of three churches located along the Buffalo River about fifteen miles northeast of Moorhead. The nearest town is Glyndon, not too far from Perley where I had spent the former summer.

I cannot adequately describe my thoughts and feelings I experienced at that time. It takes an earthquake or a tornado to keep me awake, but that night I did not sleep. I was happy in my decision and yet the seriousness of the situation weighed heavily upon me. My life passed in review before me, step by step. My Shepherd certainly had led me to still waters and green pastures. Early the next day I wrote a letter to my parents telling them of the two calls I had received, of my vow, and of my decision.

Miss Carrie Olson, who had responded to my interest in her, came to Minneapolis and was employed as a practical obstetrical nurse by Dr. Disen, who was her cousin. Some of the young men at the seminary, who had known her at St. Olaf College, again sought her attention and pursued her as they had in Northfield, especially the one who seemed to have been favored by her back then. But by the early spring of 1898, almost three years since college days, my courage and aplomb had developed apace and I also occupied some of her time. We met more and more frequently at parties and other affairs; I invited her out to concerts, recitals, and even to a few grand operas. One evening, after we had attended some entertainment, we talked about various St. Olaf couples. I grasped my opportunity and suggested that the two of us should add ourselves to the list. Carrie was not ready to give her consent, but I had reason to feel hopeful, and my prospects were further strengthened when I saw her again the following evening. Just at that time she went home to Taylor, Jackson County, Wisconsin, where her parents maintained a large farm. But before she departed I asked her to marry me and to let me know her decision before I met the ordination board on June 11th. On June 10th I received a telegram from her father, George Olson, which read, "You may answer the board in the affirmative."

My mother had arrived for my ordination and was in my room when the telegram arrived. I showed it to her and she asked me what it meant. I said, "It means that I am engaged to the finest girl I have ever met, and the mystery is, why would she want me?" She said that any girl ought to be glad to get me. I told my mother all about Carrie. When I finished my lengthy and detailed recital, she said, "You have always been sensible; I hope you are level-headed in this matter, too." Later, when she met Carrie, she was assured that I was not only sensible but lucky, too.

The next day my friend and classmate, Glesne, who was betrothed, told me that the ordination board would ask each of us if we were engaged to be married. The board members knew of the blessings of marriage and that ministers who were settled down did a better job in their parishes. I told him he needn't worry about it. He expressed regret that I was footloose, and urged me to propose to Carrie Olson. "She has always spoken highly of you and I think you should try, anyway, because she might say yes. She's a peach and you know there are few girls like her."

I thought I had withheld my secret long enough and told him my good news. He was surprised and delighted, patted me on the back, and was one wide grin. As Glesne had foretold, the ordination committee asked me if I was engaged. I told the group the same news I had given Ole. They wanted to know when the event had occurred. Very slowly, as if I was trying to remember the date, I said, "About twenty four hours ago." I think that dignified group never experienced such a hearty laugh before or since.

The examinations, which covered all three years of seminary attendance, were difficult and thorough. Each candidate prepared a sermon in written form which was closely studied and scrutinized by the board members. If it was pronounced acceptable, the candidate was then required to conduct a service and preach that sermon to students and faculty. We were required to take written examinations covering each course we had studied during the three years followed by oral examinations over the same material. The latter ordeal was conducted *in camera*. One at a time, we were ushered into a room and assigned a chair facing a semi-circle of a dozen professors and members of the ordination committee. First, the faculty members asked me detailed questions which I answered satisfactorily. Then I was handed a Bible and asked to read a portion of the Old Testament in Hebrew, then a section of the New Testament in Greek, both of which I was required to translate and explain. When the professors finished their examination of me, the other members of the board were asked if they had any questions. I was the last of the four candidates who had been examined that afternoon and everyone was tired. They pronounced themselves satisfied, much to my relief.

One part of the test that afternoon had been on church history. I can't explain it but I had had a strong hunch or feeling that I would be asked to expatiate on the Protestant Reformation when we came to that area of study. I admit I was never keenly interested in historic names or dates, but I had spent a great deal of time and effort in studying all aspects of the Reformation. I had soaked myself in the subject and was delighted, although not particularly surprised because of my strong intuition, when Dr. Lund said, "Kildahl, will you tell us about the Lutheran Reformation?" I took a few moments to organize my thoughts and then launched into a detailed lecture on the subject that lasted fifteen or twenty minutes. It was a hot day and some of the board members were almost asleep, but as I warmed to my subject they sat up and were wide awake before I finished. I was gratified to see some of them nod to each other as if signaling their satisfaction with my recitation. My happy presentiment or hunch had been amazingly accurate.

I felt sorry for Wallom. He was a particular friend of mine, had a fine memory, and knew much more about church history than I did, but he was given an examination subject that we had studied almost three years earlier, a subject that was rather insignificant. He had every reason to feel confident he could pass the test with flying colors, but the easily forgettable, obscure subject matter stunned him, muted him, and he could not answer, he told me, for some time, but finally mustered his resources enough to find an answer that satisfied the ordination board. It was a great relief for all the candidates to be finished with the examinations. We were all curious to know the outcome of our ordeal and our ranking in the class.

I was delighted, of course, to find that I had passed all the examinations, and was in effect, certified for ordination.

I was somewhat dumbfounded to discover that I was to be graduated "saerdales duelig," the Norwegian equivalent of Summa Cum Laude. The term in Norwegian means "exceptionally capable." I had worked hard, long, and diligently. In my heart of hearts I felt the distinction was justified and fairly won as did others in the class for there was not a hint of envy or jealousy expressed by my classmates.

Views of the Maza farm, circa 1900.

32

ORDINATION, MARRIAGE, AND EVER AFTER

The evening before the ordination ceremony and services were to take place, Mother, who had come from Maza for the event, asked me if Rev. Muus planned to be in attendance. I told her he not only was in Minneapolis for the ordination but was living in the same hotel where she was staying. She was eager to see him but her ailments were acting up and it was painful for her to walk. She felt she should visit him but she was in pain and simply could not leave her room. I told her not to worry about it, that I would find Rev. Muus and bring him to her. I went to his room, knocked, and when he opened his door, he recognized me, although it had been many years since we had seen each other. He was surprised and pleased to know that my mother was in the same hotel and readily agreed to accompany me to her room. When I opened the door he entered and saw her sitting on the other side of the room. He stopped, looked intently at her for a few moments, then went to her and took her hand. I brought a chair for him, he sat, and, without uttering a word, he wept like a child. Soon Mother joined him in tears. It was one of the most touching scenes I have ever witnessed.

When they composed themselves they enjoyed a long visit. She reminded him of what he had said those many years before when he persuaded my parents to let Nathan go to school, that it would turn out to be a blessing, not only for my brother, but for them, too. He said, "You left Goodhue County poor and you return rich." She told him that her children had made it possible for Johan and her to have whatever they needed, but they had no riches. "Yes, you have," he said, "you have one man in the ministry and you will have another tomorrow, and that is what I call riches." That evening was the last time I saw Rev. Muus.[59]

In 1889 Nathan accepted a call to Bethlehem Church in Chicago. Bethlehem was run down, had been badly served, and was nearing the point of closing its doors for good. It was an entirely different situation from the two large congreations he had built up at Vangs and Urland Churches in Goodhue County. But Nathan felt challenged by the desolate prospects at Bethlehem and accepted. It did not take long for him to turn despair into hope, to win back parishoners who had drifted away, and infuse enthusiasm and joy in worship among the growing number of churchgoers. Soon galleries had to be built to seat overflow audiences. I'm convinced Nathan had a touch of genius as a pastor and he gave everything he had in him to that church and its growing congregation, and the people responded generously.

In 1898 the grateful congregation voted him a three-month vacation and provided ample funds to allow him and his wife, Bertha, to spend the time on an extended visit to Norway. He had arranged for a substitute pastor to serve during his absence but, at the last moment, an emergency situation arose in the man's family forcing him to cancel. Nathan needed a replacement on short notice and asked me to fill his pulpit for three months. He said he knew it would be awkward for me, but if I could possibly do it he and Bertha would be most grateful. I took the matter up with my congregations. They had been waiting for me since I had accepted their call, but representatives of the three churches agreed that a further wait until fall was a hardship they could endure, a courtesy Nathan and I appreciated.

The ordination was a serious, impressive procedure. I was proud that my mother and Rev. Muus were present to witness my consecration as a pastor in the Lutheran Church, with all the duties, obligations, powers, rights, and privileges that calling entails. When it was over, I bade my fellow ordination candidates and my mother goodbye. I looked for Rev. Muus but he had slipped away. That evening I entrained for Chicago, allowing for a two day stopover to visit Carrie at her home in Taylor, Wisconsin.

After a pleasant two days with my fiancée and her folks, I arrived in Chicago late on the Friday night prior to the Sunday on which I was to begin my work. I had cut my time too closely. I had never conducted a full, formal, ritualistic service and I knew there would be a large audience. I also knew I must do my best to measure up to my brother's superb preaching and had little time to prepare my sermon. I could do nothing that night because it was near midnight and I went to bed. Strangely, I could not sleep, a rarity with me. Frankly, I was worried. Finally, I got out of bed, knelt, told God all my troubles, and placed the responsibility on Him. I went back to bed, fell asleep immediately and actually overslept the next morning. When I awoke on that Saturday, all fear had vanished. Confidently, I prepared my sermon and readied myself for the full service before a large, expectant congregation. All went well, a harbinger of the following three months which passed swiftly and joyfully, and were richly rewarding for me and, I hope, for the congregation. When Nathan returned from abroad, I turned over the church to him in the same condition it was when he left it. My reward was excellent preparation to take over my own charge.

I finished my work in Chicago the last week of September and had ample time to gather myself together and travel to Black River Falls, county seat of Jackson County, Wisconsin, and a thriving center of commerce. I purchased some last minute clothing items, and then went on to Taylor in the western section of the county and the Olson farm nearby where, on October 5th, 1898, Carrie Emilie Olson and I were joined in matrimony. It was a fine wedding with many guests, mostly of the Olson's, in attendance. Often I have marveled at my good fortune in winning her as a bride. She has been a loving wife, a devoted mother, and a capable and accomplished partner in my work.

For a short period it was doubtful we could be married because Carrie objected to the knot being tied by the pastor of the local congregation. Evidently she and the minister had had a falling out and Carrie would not have him at the wedding, an early example of her independent spirit. Her parents feared he would be offended if the pastor from another nearby town was asked to officiate. They wanted Nathan to conduct the service but he was a resident of Illinois, not licensed or certified to perform pastoral duties in Wisconsin, according to the laws of the time. I informed the Olsons and Carrie that I had a second cousin who was a clergyman in their state. He was acceptable to Carrie and her parents which solved the problem to everyone's contentment.

My cousin was notified and he came immediately to Taylor and the farm. The wedding and reception were held on the specified day, to everyone's joy and satisfaction.

When the reception was winding down, Carrie changed, as did I, and we slipped away to Black River Falls, which was the first stop on our wedding trip, planned to be brief because we needed to be in Moorhead, and then on to my three churches, in short order. But curtailed as the honeymoon was, we did allow for a few days in Minneapolis, a few days free of obligation before assuming my pastoral duties near Glyndon on the Buffalo River.

My charge had always been served from Moorhead, but when I accepted the call from the three congregations, they decided to build a manse within the charge. An attractive location had been acquired on the west bank of the Buffalo River directly across that stream from Concordia, the largest and most centrally located of the three churches that constituted my charge. Although they had waited for me three months longer than they initially had expected, and those months were the best building period of the year, little work had been done on the parsonage. The congregations promptly voted and raised funds for renting an apartment in Moorhead to shelter us over the winter. We arrived there early on a rather cold morning that was also dark and dreary. I hailed a taxi and told the driver to take us to the warmest hotel in town. He drove for five to ten minutes and then stopped his horse and cab in front of a hotel located just a block from the depot. Even Moorhead had its share of city slickers!

On Sunday morning, October 16th, I was installed by Circuit President Rev. Wold. That service was most impressive. The large church was filled to capacity and the feeling of responsibility in being installed as the pastor of that multitude was almost overwhelming. They were my people to instruct, lead, inspire, shepherd, and save while they were in my care in this parish. Even though I had lived through many and varied experiences and had bolstered my confidence during the past summer, I felt humble and unequal to the task confronting me. Ambivalently, I was thankful to God for the assurance of His leadership, and the promise that as my day was, so would my strength be.

Winter-trapped in Moorhead, so to speak, I could not spend the time I wished with my parishoners and to occupy my hours I conducted a class in religion at Concoria College. When we were settled in the new parsonage the following summer, everyone seemed overjoyed to have Carrie and me living among them and expressed their happiness by sharing their food and fuel with us. In keeping with the custom among rural parishes at that time, there was hardly a beef butchered within a reasonable distance that was not shared with us. Butter, eggs, cream, vegetables, and dressed poultry were brought as gifts. The people were generous to a fault and often I felt embarrassed. One neighbor placed a cow in our barn and told us we could milk her until she dried up and then he would replace her with another. A second kept us supplied with oats for the horse and a third kept us in firewood. One congregation paid for our buggy and another for the harness. During the two years we remained on the Buffalo River near Glyndon, the goodness and generosity of the parishioners never ceased. We will, always be appreciative of them for their kindness and devotion to us. May God forever bless those wonderful people and hold them in His hand.

Antiochia Church and Cemetary,
near Churchs Ferry, North Dakota

Gravestone of Johan and Nicoline Kildahl
Antiochia Cemetary.

My father's reminiscences of his youth and early manhood end, appropriately, with his year of culmination. He attained three great goals in 1898: ordination, marriage, and installation as a full-fledged pastor. Before that pivotal year, although he turned 33 in 1898 and was old compared to other students, he had striven like a youth both on the land and in the classroom to fulfill his dreams. Thereafter he assumed the duties of a husband, a pastor of three churches, and soon, a father. The days of his youth and early manhood were truly finished as he and his bride were on the threshold of a new and different life together.

My father did include, in his memoirs, tributes to the two greatest men (other than Nathan) who touched his life, Rev. Muus and Professor Mohn. He also describes actions he took to memorialize the former and shelter the family of the latter following his death in 1899. Those initiatives were, first, to raise money to place appropriate monuments to Rev. Muus over his grave in Trondhjem and at Holden where the pioneer pastor had done his work for forty years in Minnesota. The latter was not put in place until 1935; it took a long time but Father lived to see the work done. He had been unhappy since Rev. Muus's death in 1900 with the lack of recognition accorded the latter for his tireless, magnificent work among settlers covering an area equal to that of Denmark, and which now contains over 150 congregations. He determined to do something about it and he accomplished his goal.

The second action was on behalf of the widow and children of Professor Mohn following his death in 1899. At a meeting of St. Olaf alumni just before Professor Mohn's death, the group agreed with Dad's motion to raise money to buy land and build a home for the Mohn family. It was done. On November 6th, 1900, exactly one year after the motion was adopted, the keys and deed were turned over to Mrs. Mohn.

Father wrote:

Nothing I have done has given me as much real pleasure. Professor Mohn took our family under his protection and care when we lived in Northfield. I, with the help of many others, had the opportunity to repay Mrs. Mohn, if not her husband, by providing a home for her and her children that was free, clear, and permanently theirs.

      Before describing my father's career and my parents' growing family, a few words need to be added regarding N. Johanna Kildahl, (Aunt Jo.) I have described above how, through perseverance and diligent study, she earned her Ph.D. from the University of Chicago in 1909. Unfortunately, Andrew, who had consolidated the land and operated the farm efficiently and successfully for twenty years, died in 1908. Matilda was married and lived elsewhere and Nathan, my father, and Nils were all busy with their own lives. Aunt Jo had no chance for a career in those circumstances. She had never married and spinster daughters were expected to care for their aging parents. A born scholar, fascinated with botany and biology, she gave up hopes for a life of her own and returned home to care for Nicoline and Johan, and supervise the operation of the farm.

      Both parents were from long-lived families. Johan lived until March 7th, 1916, age 96½ years. Nicoline followed him on November 9th, 1919, age 92. Aunt Jo was then 52 years old and spent the remainder of her long life on an ever-diminishing acreage near Maza during growing and harvesting seasons, and in Chicago during the winter months. She lived the longest of all the Kildahl siblings, outdoing even her parents. She died during July, 1967 in Chicago, less than two months short of having lived a full century. When she became very old she lived in the Illinois city the year around.

      My parents resided in the Glyndon, Minnesota area, serving the three Buffalo River congregations, for two years. In 1899, my oldest brother, Caleb Johan, was born in Moorhead. In 1900 Father accepted a call to be pastor of Covenant Lutheran in Chicago. He may have received that call as a direct result of his work at Bethlehem Lutheran Church while he was substituting for Nathan in 1898 as described earlier in this narrative. Although my father's youthful ambition and lifelong desire was to be a pulpit preacher, the burgeoning church and his abilities destined him to be an administrator most of his career. He felt it was his duty to relinquish his preferences in favor of the church's needs, and consequently, his tenure as pastor at Covenant was brief; his administrative skills were required elsewhere in Chicago. In 1902 the United Norwegian Lutheran Church asked him to become Rector (Superintendent) of Lutheran Deaconess Home (Hospital); He and the congregation of Covenant reluctantly parted company. He remained at Deaconess as Rector until 1912.

During the twelve years my parents and their growing family lived in Chicago, my father, in addition to his pastoral or administrative duties, was editor, first of *The Children's Companion* (1900-1904) and second, *The Deaconess Magazine* (1909-1912.) Also, during that span of years, all my other brothers and sisters were born, but Caleb Johan, age 8, succumbed to a throat infection in 1907. Before the miracles of modern medicine provided preventatives or cures for childhood diseases, premature death was an all-too-frequent occurrence in many households. Large families were the rule to compensate for probable childhood deaths; it was a grim fact of life. Nevertheless, Caleb's early demise was a bitter blow to my parents, especially to my father, who had great difficulty in accepting my brother's passing. My mother later told me he never fully recovered from that loss. Caleb was his first-born, the apple of his eye, and he had high hopes and plans for him— perhaps too high, and the letdown was a blow from which he never completely recovered, but he was helped by the presence of other children already born and yet to come. The first was Nicoline Clara, born March 5th, 1901, followed by George Olson on March 20th, 1903, and Phoebe Dorothy on July 20th, 1905. Caleb's demise in 1907, coupled with worry over his illness and heartbreak at his passing brought on a miscarriage that year. However, a new baby, Harold B. Jr., was born May 15th, 1909 and Phillip Andrew, still another, saw the light of day on June 13th, 1912. There is nothing like a houseful of children to banish gloom and soften sorrow, and that proved to be the case with my parents and older siblings.

Late in 1912 a call came to my father to be pastor of Our Savior's Lutheran Church in Milwaukee. Both of my parents wished to leave Chicago with its memories of Caleb and Dad accepted the call to Our Savior's. Earlier that year, during the summer, the family had vacationed on Prairie Lake, near Chetek, Wisconsin, and enjoyed the time spent in that growing resort area. They returned each summer and rented a cottage on the same lake until 1916.

In the latter year, Father's even tenor of life as a pulpit minister was again disrupted by the needs of the United Norwegian Lutheran Church. He was called to be Rector of Thomas and Fairview Hospitals in Minneapolis. He accepted the new assignment although, I'm sure, his wish was to remain at Our Savior's. Before the call to Minneapolis came, during the summer of 1916, he, and the older boys, built a cottage of their own on Prairie Lake. Not possessed of much money, he implemented a brilliant idea that would allow him to obtain the necessary building materials at minimum cost. He went to a wrecking yard, selected about a hundred paint-encrusted, discarded house doors, mostly unglazed, paid 25¢ for each of them, had them put on a flat car, and shipped to Chetek. There, employing his not inconsiderable carpentry skills, he cleaned, them, put up 2" by 4" studdings, and used the doors as the walls of the new cottage. He even used doors that were glazed as partitions between living and dining room. The result was a 40' by 40' cottage that became known as "the house of doors." It remained in the family until 1947, a unique structure. To catch as much lake breeze as possible, Father invented a hinged window that folded up overhead, out of the way, and allowed one entire 40' lakefront wall to be screened and open to the air as well as about half of another wall. The result was an amazingly cool house even in the hottest times of the year. The family summered at "Fairhaven" and Father was with us during his month of vacation and on weekends when his work permitted.

Late in 1916 the family moved to Minneapolis where my father assumed his new duties at the hospitals as Rector. He was not to remain in that position very long. On June 9th, 1917, the Norwegain Lutheran Church of America came into existence through the merger of the United Norwegian Lutheran Church with a number of other synods. The tendency of Lutheran church bodies to grow and merge, begun in 1890, had reached another level, and the process has continued to the present time. The new church organization designated Minneapolis as its national headquarters, and elected Rev. H. A. 0. Stub as its first president. He, knowing of my father's experience as an administrator both in Chicago and now in Minneapolis, and valuing his acquired skill, appointed him Executive Secretary of the new church organization's Board of Charities, with offices in the headquarters building, Augsburg Publishing House.

When the family came to Minneapolis in 1916, a large home was rented on Longfellow Avenue, and in that house, on my brother George's fourteenth birthday, March 20th, 1917, the youngest child of the family was born. He is the editor of these memoirs and author of this Afterword, Erling Eugene Oulie (a family name of my mother's forebears.) Of seven children in my family, six survived to maturity, a remarkable record for the early part of this century. Scarlet fever, polio, diphtheria, galloping consumption, and a world-wide epidemic of Spanish influenza took a dreadful, frightening toll of young lives. My parents were lucky—they lost only one of their brood, but some of my brothers and sisters suffered lifelong disabilities because of childhood diseases, such as partial loss of hearing or sight or both, and weakened hearts and lungs. We owe modern medicine a great debt of gratitude for the protection now afforded against such childhood scourges.

My father's new job entailed a huge increase in responsibility because it required national supervision of; orphanages or children's' homes as they came to be known; homes for the aged; Deaconess homes and hospitals; hospices and missions; (such as for seamen in ports and the homeless everywhere) rescue homes for unmarried mothers; and agencies for finding homes for unwanted babies. All those activities and institutions were sponsored by the new church body, and to adequately do his job he had to travel a great deal mostly on trains, one of his childhood loves. Although Father's choice would have been as pastor to a congregation, his new position served a much larger, a national, congregation, and he never said "no" when the national church needed him. He found time in 1919 to write and publish a book, *His Workshop*.

When Father was 68 years old, in 1933, he stepped down after 16 years and took over as Superintendent of Coeur d'Alene Home for the Aged in Coeur d'Alene, Idaho, where he remained for four years. In 1937 my parents returned to the Twin Cities where Father had been made Executive Secretary of the Anti-Saloon League, a position he held from 1937 until 1942. He was head of the United Temperance Movement from 1942 to 1943. Repeal of the Eighteenth Amendment (Prohibition) had occurred in 1933. That meant the importance of both temperance organizations Dad had headed since 1937 was dwindling. They represented a lost cause and gradually disappeared from the scene.

During the last two years of his life he returned to his first love, and was invited to conduct worship services and preach in various churches. Since 1934, when his alma mater, St. Olaf College, bestowed on him the honorary degree, Doctor of Divinity, people tended to address him as Doctor Kildahl, but he much preferred being addressed as Reverend, a title he felt he had earned. In September, 1945, Father suffered a severe stroke, and never regained consciousness. He died in Fairview Hospital on October 4th, one day shy of his and Carrie's 47th wedding anniversary. He was 80½ years old. His widow, my mother, Carrie Emilie Olson Kildahl, continued to live in St. Paul, enjoyed her children and grandchildren, church work, Grandmothers Clubs, and other organizations, filled a long life, and followed her husband in death on January 30th, 1969, in St. Paul, at the age of 93 years and nearly five months.

Since then, all of their children, save myself, have gone the way of Caleb: George Olson on July 8th, 1978, age 75; Phoebe Dorothy (Helgeson) on October 1st, 1990, age 85; Nicoline Clara (Shalda) on November 14th, 1990, age 89: Harold B. Jr., who followed in his father's footsteps and became a Lutheran pastor, died on November 22, 1986, age 87; Phillip Andrew, died on August 2, 1995, age 83; and I am 89. I find it remarkable, not unique, surely, but certainly noteworthy, that we had an aunt, Anna Delise (Jermstad) who was born in 1847, now almost a century and a half ago. During that span of time five, almost six, generations should have had their time on earth but in our family only two have come and gone or are going, thanks to long-lived ancestors. Some individuals, of course, who survived childhood, were unlucky: the first Johanna; the first Nils; Matilda; Andrew; our brother, Caleb. Our Aunt Anna Delise, who seemed to drop out of the family and of whom little is written in my father's memoirs, died in 1926, age 79.

More than two millenia ago a wise man wrote, "Those who have torches will pass them on to others." My father had a torch. Somehow, I know not how, that torch, (at least a few live embers from it,) was entrusted to my care. I can do nothing less than pass it on to others.

Erling Eugene Kildahl
June 25th, 1991

Erling E. Kildahl, the youngest child of the author, is a 1940 graduate of Jamestown College and holds a Master of Theater Arts from Pasadena Playhouse College of Theater. (1946) He was a member of the directing and instructional staff at the Playhouse from 1946 to 1948, and a Director and Professor of Speech and Theater at Purdue University from 1948 to 1981. When he retired in the latter year he was made Professor Emeritus. He resides in Lexington, KY.

ENDNOTES

1. My grandfather, Johan Kildahl, was one of four brothers. Each had a different surname: The other three were Ingebrigt Kildal, Daniel Kaldahl, and Peter Kaldal. My father offers no explanation for this anomaly.

2. Rev. Bernt J. I. Muus (1832-1900) was born in Namdalen, Norway. He emigrated in 1859 to Goodhue County and became a legendary pioneer pastor who at one time served 28 congregations. He founded St. Olaf School (later College) in Northfield in 1874 with the aid of Rev. Nils A. Quammen of Farmington.

3. The present location of Johan Kildahl's travel diary is unknown.

4. I have not found Leon on a map. It is, however, the name of a township in Goodhue County.

5. The basket is now lost.

6. Coarsely ground wheat mixed with bran.

7. Washtado (or Wastedo,) no longer exists as a town, although a school and Leon township hall remain

8. Hader lives and thrives.

9. Urland Lutheran Church, a few miles southwest of Cannon Falls, Minnesota, is not only still in existence, but very much in use. My father (the author) and mother are interred in its churchyard.

10. "The Mechanical Resuscitator" seems to have approximated the idea of acupuncture, an oriental technique, which has become a widely employed medical procedure in the United States in recent years.

11. And again, later in the century, popularized by Dr. Norman Vincent Peale and his *The Power of Positive Thinking*, which led on to wide interest in holistic medicine which asserts the mind's effect on the body

12. This meticulous and difficult technique was even then being replaced by the balloon-frame house which supported its roof—and created its stability—not on brick or stone, but on 2 × 4s set 16 inches apart, a much easier method of construction and generally used today. This method is called stud framing.

13. Holden, the name of the church, was given to the school.

14. Aspelund, if it still exists, has no post office.

15. This church body was organized in 1917 from three smaller organized Lutheran groups. Through a series of mergers it is now part of the Evangelical Lutheran Church in America.

16. The Cannon River.

17. In slightly altered form, this chapter, titled "The Northfield Bank Raid," was published in *Journal of the West*, Vol. XXIII, No. 3 (July, 1989) pp. 67-72. Reprinted with permission.

18. The Chicago, Milwaukee, and St. Paul Railroad.

19. Joseph Allen, denied access to the bank while the raid was in progress, became suspicious and raised the alarm. Only then were residents told to go inside and firearms discharged into the air.

20. My father was misinformed. Frank James killed Mr. Heywood.

21. The innocent victim's name was Nicholas Gustavson.

22. Dundas flourishes and boasts a post office.

23. This story is probably apocryphal.

24. The farmer's name was Sorbel, but there is good reason for name confusion.

25. The boy's true name was Asle Oscar Sorbel.

26. I quote from a letter sent me by Caroline M. de Mauriac, Executive Director of the Northfield Historical Society: "We had not heard before ... that the Sorbel boy was offered a free education at the University of Minnesota." She continues: "Asle Oscar Sorbel ... changed his name to Oscar Oleson Suborn to avoid possible reprisals from any friends of the gang that were captured because of him. His name has been reported in a number of different forms; Osborn being only one of many. He finally made his role in the capture of the raiders known in 1929; he was living in South Dakota. He was making a living as a Veterinarian at that time so it is possible that he may have taken the state of Minnesota up on its offer, but attended the university under an assumed name." Young Sorbel's fears leading to disappearance and subterfuge accounts for my father's ignorance herein.

27. Both Miller's and Chadwell's bodies were exhumed by Dr. Wheeler and taken to his Michigan medical school, but Miller's remains were claimed by relatives for reburial near his home in the South. Dr. Wheeler kept Chadwell's skeleton, as my father was told, until it and the office building were destroyed by fire around 1900.

28. People still come to view the site of Jesse James's ill fated bank raid.

29. Coopers made or repaired wooden tubs, kegs, and barrels.

30. See endnote 1 regarding family surnames.

31. See p. 31

32. Rev. Thorbjørn N. Mohn, first president of St. Olaf School and College (1874-1899;) founding pastor, St. John's Lutheran Church,Northfield.

33. My father does not disclose the name of the doctor, if there was one, who administered his mother's treatments. It is possible Matilda, who was quick and clever, learned the procedure and did it herself.

34. Laths are narrow, thin strips of wood used to make a supporting basis for plaster, shingles, slates, or tiles. Wood laths are seldom, if ever, used today.

35. Rev. Aaberg was a pastor among Norwegian Lutheran settlers in Ramsey, Benson, Rolette, Bottineau, and Ward counties in the territory that became North Dakota in 1889. He founded Aaberg Academy in Devils Lake in 1888. It closed in 1903.

36. In 1937 or 38, I was a guest at a rural wedding in northeastern North Dakota. The libation served at the reception consisted of five gallons of pure grain alcohol mixed with a bit of pink coloring, dipped from a clean, galvanized wash tub containing a fifty pound chunk of ice. The results from its consumption were similar to those described by my father. I had one sip of that poison and decided I'd rather live. Old customs die hard.

37. James Jerome Hill (1838-1916), American financier and railroad magnate, was admiringly called "The Empire Builder." He promoted and financed the construction of the Great Northern Railroad. In the 20th century its finest limited to the Pacific coast was given that name in his honor.

38. Founded in 1867 when an Indian reservation was established. Named for Gen. Joseph Gilbert Totten (1788-1864) former Chief, Eng. Corps, U.S. Army.

39. Some success has attended recent efforts to restore, the lake.

40. The late 1920s or early 30s.

41. Andrew's expectations were justified. When the Northern Pacific R. R. extended its system north from Jamestown, the village of Maza came into existence only two to three miles from the family's farm.

42. The lake bed east of my family's former land holdings is now named Lake Alice, and is smaller than my father's description would lead the reader to expect. No island in Lake Alice is recorded in plat maps or descriptions of the township or Ramsey County dating back to the first decade of this century. Mr. Gordon Cowan, who lives and farms near Churchs Ferry, theorized to me that in the 1880s the lake was much larger and that a ridge, east of the present bed of Lake Alice, was the island my father describes. I believe his conjecture is correct. Over the years, the requirements of agriculture and growing human water use have caused all lakes in the area to shrink or disappear. The entire lake complex, dry except for a period following heavy rains, is now a Federal Wildlife Refuge.

43. See footnote 42.

44. Built in 1821, on the site of an earlier trading post, by the Hudson's Bay Co. of Canada. It is at the junction of the Assiniboine and Red rivers, and is now the location of the city of Winnipeg, Manitoba.

45. The bones were probably ground up, made into bone meal, and sold as fertilizer.

46. They were probably reservation Sioux. My father does not specify.

47. In 1888, after the permanent home was built, this solid stable was replaced with a proper barn

48. I.e., 48° 22' north latitude. There are 60 minutes, or 60 surveying lines, between major parallels such as the 48th and 49th which, for the most part, marks the boundary between the United States and Canada.

49. Not noticeable on major highways or interstates.

50. At the time these memoirs were written, this was the name of a popular comic strip involving a stringbean "Mutt" and a short "Jeff."

51. Neither Island Lake nor Plunder, if existing, have post offices.

52. see note #35.

53. Not far from the junction of U.S. Highways 2 and 281, the church, in 1990, was regularly used for services, well maintained, and open to all.

54. See "Origin of the Rope Corral," by Nils Kildahl in *The Bit and Spur*, March, 1948, p.11.

55. World War I.

56. Nils died in August, 1948.

57. Vangs Church, thrives with an active congregation.

58. Halver T. Ytterboe (1857–1904) was unwavering in his dedication and devotion to St. Olaf College. A building on campus is named for him.

59. Rev. Muus retired from his forty-year ministry in 1899, burnt out, as is said today. He went home to Norway and on May 25th, 1900, he died. He is buried beside his brother near the Cathedral in Trondhjem.

CPSIA information can be obtained
at www.ICGtesting.com
Printed in the USA
LVHW050357161122
733223LV00005B/692